ARCHAEOLOGY: MYTH AND REALITY

Readings from

SCIENTIFIC AMERICAN

ARCHAEOLOGY: MYTH AND REALITY

With an Introduction by

Jeremy A. Sabloff
University of New Mexico

W. H. Freeman and Company
San Francisco

Most of the SCIENTIFIC AMERICAN articles in *Archaeology: Myth and Reality* are available as separate Offprints. For a complete list of articles now available as Offprints, write to W. H. Freeman and Company, 660 Market Street, San Francisco, California 94104.

Library of Congress Cataloging in Publication Data

Main entry under title:

Archaeology: myth and reality: readings from Scientific American.

Bibliography: p.
Includes index.
Contents: The Hopewell cult / Prufer—Stonehenge / Hawkes—Carbon 14 and the prehistory of Europe / Renfrew—[etc.]
1. Archaeology—Addresses, essays, lectures.
2. Man, Prehistoric—Addresses, essays, lectures.
3. Civilization, Ancient—Addresses, essays, lectures.
4. Antiquities—Addresses, essays, lectures.
I. Sabloff, Jeremy A. II. Scientific American.
CC173.A73 930.1 81–17296
ISBN 0–7167–1394–2 AACR2
ISBN 0–7167–1395–0 (pbk.)

Printed in the United States of America

9 8 7 6 5 4 3 2 1 KP 0 8 9 8 7 6 5 4 3 2

PREFACE

We are so used to machines we forget what man can do on his own.

Peter White

The widespread popular acceptance of pseudoarchaeological ideas may partly be due to the fact that archaeologists have been remiss in communicating to the public how they perform research, analysis, and interpretation. Just as one does not become a chemist by looking at water, one cannot become an archaeologist merely by looking at ancient monuments or even by digging at an archaeological site. While mythologizing about the past obviously has great appeal to the general public, pseudoarchaeology has not been nearly as successful as professional archaeology in consistently reconstructing and explaining the past. When two belief systems clash, the extremists of both persuasions will find it difficult to communicate with each other effectively, but reasonable individuals can and should try to explain their viewpoints to others. Scientific archaeologists have an important message to communicate, one which, if properly communicated, should persuade general readers of its efficacy and utility.

In examining the pseudoarchaeological literature on ancient phenomena, it immediately becomes clear that professional archaeologists and pseudoarchaeologists have different belief systems and different methods of constructing theories. For example, the scientific method used by professional archaeologists requires a procedure of hypothesis formulation and testing, whereas pseudoarchaeologists offer conjectures that archaeologists see as unproven or unprovable. Pseudoarcheologists also tend to discuss objects or ideas out of context, whereas archaeologists always attempt to view all cultural phenomena in their specific cultural contexts.

Scientific American has been a leader in bringing scientific advances to the attention of the interested public. In the area of archaeology, it has been particularly effective in communicating new discoveries and reputable interpretations. This book is a further contribution to this end. However, the issues raised in the Introduction—namely, the differences between professional archaeological and pseudoarchaeological interpretations of the archaeological record—have not usually been explicitly addressed in the pages of *Scientific American*.

I have chosen seven articles from *Scientific American* that offer professional views on ancient phenomena—Stonehenge, the pyramids of Egypt and Mexico, the Hopewell phenomenon, and the Nazca desert markings. These phenomena have also been treated sensationally by a variety of pseudoarchaeological writers. Generally speaking, most of these articles were not written specifically to counter pseudoscientific popularizations but were written primarily to present new data and interpretations. These articles are reprinted here in order to provide the reader with examples of professional perspectives on these topics. In my Introduction, I relate these professional views to some of the pseudoarchaeological literature and show how current scientific knowledge fails to support the popularized pseudoarchaeological contentions. Moreover, I briefly explain how professional archaeological methods differ from the methods of pseudoarchaeologists and how pseudoarchaeologists disregard the scientific method.

The articles in this volume exemplify the intellectual procedures archaeologists use to analyze, explain, and describe the past. Application of these procedures has produced reasonable interpretations of ancient phenomena that are more plausible than those offered by pseudoarchaeologists. I sincerely hope that both believers and doubters of the views of contemporary sensationalist writers will be sufficiently motivated by my discussion and by the *Scientific American* articles to delve more deeply into the current state of knowledge about Stonehenge, the Egyptian and Mexican pyramids, and the desert markings on the plains of Nazca. It is my firm belief that, as the general public gains a better understanding of the methods and results of professional archaeologists, they will be less susceptible to unwarranted and dubious claims about the "mysteries of the past."

Given the relatively short length of my Introduction to this set of readings, I have not been able to discuss in detail the nature of specific pseudoarchaeological claims about ancient phenomena, the archaeological arguments against such claims, and the general philosophical inadequacies of various pseudoarchaeological approaches. A list of Selected Readings is provided at the end of my introductory essay to guide readers to the sources that provided the data for my necessarily abbreviated discussions.

I would like to express my deep gratitude to my wife, Paula L. W. Sabloff, for her editorial aid and support, to C. C. Lamberg-Karlovsky for suggesting the title of this book, and to Margaret W. Conkey for her detailed suggestions for improving the clarity of my introductory remarks.

January 1982 Jeremy A. Sabloff

CONTENTS

Introduction 1

I THE CHANGING NATURE OF ANTHROPOLOGICAL ARCHAEOLOGY

PRUFER 1 The Hopewell Cult 29

II STONEHENGE

HAWKES 2 Stonehenge 39
RENFREW 3 Carbon 14 and the Prehistory of Europe 47
DANIEL 4 Megalithic Monuments 56

III LINES IN THE PERUVIAN DESERT

ISBELL 5 The Prehistoric Ground Drawings of Peru 69

IV PYRAMIDS

EMERY 6 The Tombs of the First Pharaohs 78
MILLON 7 Teotihuacán 85

Bibliographies 97
Index 99

Note on cross-references to SCIENTIFIC AMERICAN *articles:* Articles included in this book are referred to by title and page number; articles not included in this book but available as Offprints are referred to by title and offprint number; articles not included in this book and not available as Offprints are referred to by title and date of publication.

ARCHAEOLOGY: MYTH AND REALITY

INTRODUCTION

There is a vast untapped popular interest in the deepest scientific questions. For many people, the shoddily thought out doctrines of borderline science are the closest approximation to comprehensible science readily available. The popularity of borderline science is a rebuke to the schools, the press and commercial television for their sparse, unimaginative and ineffective efforts at science education; and to us scientists, for doing so little to popularize our subject.

Carl Sagan

One of the great insights of the science of anthropology is an appreciation for the diversity of human cultures and the magnitude of their accomplishments in a wide variety of environments. Archaeologists, like anthropologists, gain immense respect for the ability of ancient peoples to adapt to difficult environments and to create major cultural achievements, whose remains often endure for centuries or millennia. In contrast, pseudoarchaeologists—nonspecialists who write about archaeological topics without adhering to the tenets of scientific research, analysis, and interpretation—show little or no anthropological perspective on human achievements. They often seem to start with the premise that a given culture could not have created or built a given monument; therefore, some other beings—from across the oceans, under the oceans, or outer space—must have provided the impetus necessary for creation.

In some cases, this lack of an anthropological perspective appears to be a kind of naive racism. An example of this sort of thinking would be the assumption that the Maya—as Indians—were incapable of perfecting a sophisticated writing and numerical system, and therefore some Old World people or extraterrestrial being must have taught the Maya everything they knew. In other cases, pseudoarchaeologists simply seem to be unaware of the existence of the comparative anthropological and archaeological literature and the extensive data on local or regional chronologies. Pseudoarchaeologists often fail to understand the role of diffusion (as opposed to independent invention) in cultural change. For instance, the ancient Egyptians had virtually ceased to build pyramids several millennia before pyramids were built at Teotihuacán in Mexico, yet a few writers credit the Egyptians with stimulating the creation of the Mexican structures. Many so-called mysteries are readily explainable when examined in the context of a local sequence of development or a regional matrix of cultures. A greater public awareness of the insights of anthropology might cause many pseudoarchaeologists to rewrite their books, or at least would enable general readers to be more critical when reading pseudoarchaeological works.

THE CHANGING NATURE OF ANTHROPOLOGICAL ARCHAEOLOGY

Pseudoarchaeologists are not only unaware of the anthropological perspective, they also have little understanding of the nature of the discipline of archaeology today. Although archaeology receives substantial media coverage, the image most people have of archaeology is often totally at variance with the true nature of the discipline. Professional anthropological archaeologists today do not search for art objects for their market value or dig up relics for their spectacular appeal. Moreover, they are not solely interested in describing the past. The media image of archaeology that emphasizes the search for mysterious treasure or concern with a particular object that is the link with a lost civilization does a disservice to archaeology and to the general public as well. Although some archaeologists in the past did pursue these goals, contemporary anthropological archaeologists are primarily interested in explaining cultural development and change. Archaeologists are now as interested in questions of how and why as in questions of what, when, and where, although all these questions are closely related and each is important to archaeological research. Perhaps archaeologist Charles L. Redman (1973, p. 20) put it best when he said that "today's archaeologist is a social scientist who studies human behavior and social organization by analyzing artifacts of past human activities." This new emphasis in the archaeological discipline has been accompanied by a host of changes in methods, techniques, and general perspectives in viewing the study of the past.

At least seven factors have played crucial roles in the development of the "new archaeology." First, like many other social scientists, archaeologists now view a culture as a system comprising many interrelated subsystems, such as technology, political structure, economy, religion, and the like. Archaeologists are interested in the nature of interactions among the different subsystems—how a change in one subsystem affects the other subsystems. For example, an increase in population might lead to attempts to increase agricultural production, which in turn might affect how food is distributed, the kinds of tools needed to work the fields, and so on. Contemporary archaeologists seek to determine whether there are predictable regularities in these interactions.

Second, and closely related to systems thinking, is the relatively new concern with the interaction between a culture and its physical environment—animals, plants, minerals, weather, and the like. Archaeologists currently are applying ecological and ecosystemic models to investigate whether the ecological principles that govern the interactions of plants, animals, and the nonliving world might help explain how human populations are influenced by their environments, and vice versa.

Third is the attempt by archaeologists to build a cultural evolutionary theory analogous to modern biological evolutionary theory. Archaeologists would like to test general propositions that are well accepted in the biological theory of evolution, such as that a highly specialized form of life is relatively more likely to become extinct than a nonspecialized one, against the record of human cultural development. Do human cultures develop according to general principles? Are these analogous to the principles that govern the biological evolution of other animals? Archaeologists are now beginning to ask such questions and test hypotheses about human cultural evolution.

Fourth, many archaeologists are now concentrating their attention on the variability in the archaeological record. Archaeologists hope to understand the roles that different cultural subsystems play in adapting a human population to its environment, and they hope to associate material remains (pottery, architecture, etc.) with these different subsystems. This approach is in marked contrast to the older view that emphasized homogeneity in culture and defined cultures in terms of a series of traits (trait lists), such as house form, place of burial, pottery style, and the like. Changes in these traits were used to mark different time periods, while similar traits in two different regions were assumed to indicate that at least one aspect of the culture in one region had spread (diffused) to the other. The actual mechanism of diffusion, such as trade or migration, often was left unspecified. By considering a culture as a set of subsystems that allows variability, archaeologists began to see that differences, say, in pottery or arrowheads, could represent functional differences rather than chronological differences. For example, archaeologists used to believe that stone points of various kinds, which are found in European caves and date to part of the Paleolithic period, represented different chronological eras. More recent evidence indicates that some of these points may be functionally different components of a contemporary "tool kit." That is, one kind was used for scraping hides, another for cutting wood, and so on. The concept of variability within a culture recognizes the fact that changes within the many subsystems of a culture occur at different rates and in response to various changes in the environment.

Fifth, archaeologists are becoming much more sophisticated in their interpretations of the archaeological record and in their use of a variety of new techniques for recovering and analyzing this record. Such techniques as radiocarbon dating permit archaeologists to assign absolute dates to portions of the archaeological record. Neutron activation analyses of trace elements allow archaeologists to relate stone tools made of obsidian, for example, to the specific outcrops or quarries where these tools were manufactured. Furthermore, archaeologists, more than ever before, appreciate how the archaeological record has been transformed through time by a wide variety of natural and cultural means and is not necessarily a faithful register of past human activities.

Sixth, the growing use of computers and a wide array of scientific hardware has enabled archaeologists to obtain and manipulate data in ways that were heretofore impossible. For example, the application of computer simulation techniques makes it possible for archaeologists to model large cultural systems even when only fragmentary parts of such systems are preserved in the archaeological record.

Finally, archaeologists have begun to adopt more rigorous procedures in formulating and testing (supporting or rejecting) their hypotheses about cultural change. Assumptions are made clear; hypotheses are explicitly stated; and test implications for these hypotheses are detailed. Although for decades archaeologists have attempted to follow scientific methods in undertaking research and analysis, contemporary archaeologists insist on stricter experimental methods and interpretive procedures.

These seven factors are related and mutually reinforcing in many ways. Taken together, they have significantly changed the way many archaeologists view the study of the past and the kinds of archaeological problems they deem significant. A good case example, which clearly reveals some of the changes that have occurred in archaeological thinking, is the history of the archaeological study of the eastern United States during the period from about 100 BC to AD 600. Centered in Ohio is an ancient cultural phenomenon that has been labeled *Hopewell*. Olaf Prufer's *Scientific American* article "The Hopewell Cult" (p. 28) provides the reader with a good introduction to recent theories about the Hopewell phenomenon. But let us here briefly review two centuries of speculation about the Hopewell finds.

In the late eighteenth and early nineteenth century, as the newly formed United States pushed its frontiers to the west, reports of large earthen mounds and geometric embankments in Ohio were carried to the East Coast. Many of these large mounds were found to contain a variety of finely made artifacts, and many sites seemed to be placed at strategic locations on or near the confluence of rivers. These locations were ideally suited for modern habitation, and new towns such as Cincinnati, Marietta, and Circleville, Ohio, were built directly on top of these mound sites. As might be expected, the question of who built the mounds soon captured the public's imagination. Indeed, this question intrigued both the general public and the intellectual circles of Boston, New York, Philadelphia, and Washington, D.C. Since hard data were few, speculation ran rampant, and a wide variety of answers to the question of who built the mounds was suggested. Two major schools of thought emerged. One viewed the mounds as the products of a lost race of Moundbuilders who had created the mounds and associated artifacts and subsequently had left the eastern part of North America. Some imagined that these Moundbuilders then moved south, where they became the Toltecs or Aztecs and built the great civilizations of Mexico. The other principal position was that the ancestors of the native Americans living in the general area had built the mounds and that there was a cultural continuity from the Moundbuilders to the present-day American Indians.

The debate engaged a number of the leading intellectual and political figures of the time, the majority of whom appeared to believe in the lost race of Moundbuilders. As Robert Silverberg insightfully points out in *Mound Builders of Ancient America: The Archaeology of a Myth*, among the several forces behind the lost-race position was the political urge to deny that the modern native inhabitants had any great cultural heritage and the nationalistic desire to create a heroic past for the Americas that would rival the Classical Greek and Roman past of Europe. Opinions about the origin and fate of the Moundbuilders were wildly imaginative. Groups from the east (across the Atlantic), the west (from Asia), and the south (ancient Mexico) were proposed as sources for the lost race. Norsemen, Scythians, Aztecs, Hindustanis, or one of the Ten Lost Tribes of Israel were among the most popular candidates. As Silverberg (1968, p. 57) notes, "The dream of a lost prehistoric race in the American heartland was profoundly satisfying; and if the vanished ones had been giants, or white men, or Israelites, or Danes, or Toltecs, or great White Jewish Toltec Vikings, so much the better."

Not until the end of the nineteenth century was the lost-race hypothesis scientifically put to rest, although the Moundbuilder myth has begun to reappear in the recent publications of several writers of pseudoarchaeology. What finally convinced archaeologists and much of the public that ancestors of native American Indians had built the mounds was the accumulation of careful field data and scholarly research that showed the continuity of cultures from ancient through historic times. Between the surveys of Squier and Davis in the 1840s and the extensive research and excavations of Cyrus Thomas in the latter part of the century, archaeology emerged as a scientific profession with full-time, trained practitioners. As more researchers began using more sophisticated field methods in the early decades of this century, archaeologists were able to classify many of the mounds into a cultural grouping, which was labeled the *Hopewell culture*.

Scholars were able to define the Hopewell culture on the basis of architecture, artifacts, and burial practices. Henry C. Shetrone, for example, defined Hopewell (1920, p. 156) on the basis of the following traits:

> Extensive complex earthworks of geometric forms; mounds usually low, irregularly shaped structures, often within or adjacent to the typical earthworks; burial tumuli usually cover the sites or remains of structures, varying from unpretentious enclosures of upright timbers or posts to similarly constructed buildings of large size, serving as sacred places into which the dead were taken for funeral obsequies and sepulture; cremation of the dead and disposition of their ashes in prepared graves of puddled clay the rule, though not to the exclusion of uncremated burial; sculptural art highly developed, particularly in the carving of life forms in stone; comparatively high development of the textile and factile arts, as evidence in woven cloth and fabric and in burned clay pottery ware; strikingly free use of copper, both for ornament and utility; and the extensive possession and use of materials from distant sources of supply, as mica, obsidian, quartz crystal, and galena.

Scholars concluded that the center of Hopewell culture was in Ohio. From there it spread west to Illinois and Missouri, as well as into the southeastern United States and Great Lakes areas. Sites in Ohio seemed to have most of

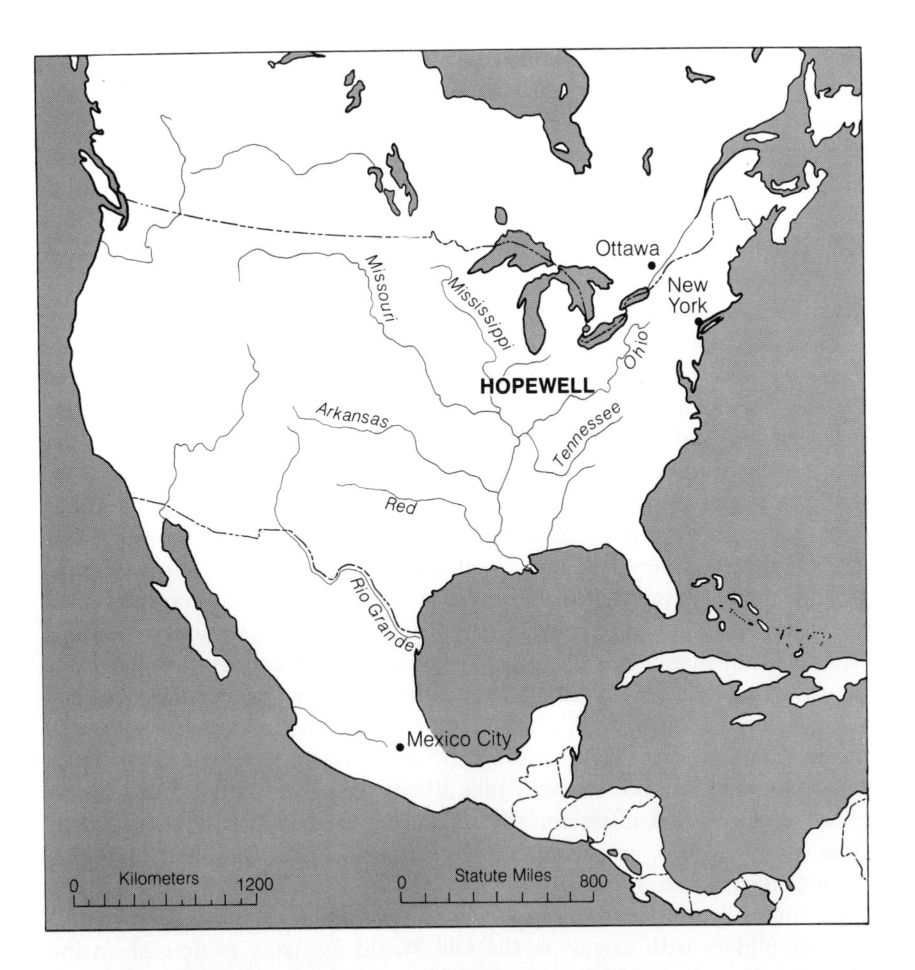

the Hopewell traits, while those farther away tended to have only a few. In some regions, one site had Hopewell traits, while others did not. The application of the radiocarbon method of dating to archaeological materials allowed archaeologists to date Hopewell from about 100 BC to AD 600.

In the late 1950s and early 1960s, archaeologists began to ask more questions of how and why and to examine more critically their assumptions. Some archaeologists identified major conceptual problems with the dominant trait-list view of the Hopewell culture. Prufer clarifies one such problem in pointing out that the definition of Hopewell culture was derived almost exclusively from data on burial mounds and not from data on habitation areas. This sampling error was similar to one made in early studies of Classic Maya civilization, which emphasized the great temples and palaces to the virtual exclusion of the relatively modest houses where the peasants lived. In other words, theories about the Hopewell culture had been based to a large extent on information about the elites of certain sites and how they were buried. New work on habitation areas in the 1960s showed that local traditions in various parts of the East were quite different, although some of the elite traits were shared.

A second set of objections to early twentieth-century views of the Hopewell phenomenon arose from archaeologists' dissatisfaction with the traditional archaeological view of culture as a relatively homogenous conglomeration of shared ideas. In the early twentieth century, archaeologists tended to view specific cultures as a series of traits shared by the members of these cultures. Comparisons among cultures were made on the basis of shared traits (pottery types, house forms, etc.), and traits were assumed to diffuse from one culture to another by an unspecified mechanism. In the Hopewell case, most of the traits were present in Ohio, but only certain ones spread to the farther reaches of the area covered by Hopewell culture. By the early 1960s, archaeologists had become dissatisfied with this traditional view and began looking at culture from a systems perspective, which, as enunciated by archaeologist Lewis R. Binford and others, emphasizes the diversity of culture. Instead of shared ideas, it emphasizes the participation of people in culture and notes that people participate differently, depending on status, occupation, and other factors. In effect, the systems perspective argues that different cultural subsystems play varied adaptive roles. Therefore, archaeologists must become concerned with correlating the material remains they discover with the different subsystems from which the objects originated.

In the case of the Hopewell culture, systems archaeologists argued that there was an *interaction sphere* that linked the elite of a number of sites in eastern North America. This interaction sphere was defined as "the prehistoric logistics network within which quantities of raw materials, finished goods, stylistic ideas, and ideological concepts circulated" (Struever, 1964, p. 89). The Hopewell interaction sphere connected sites that belonged to entirely different local and regional cultural traditions. Moreover, the interaction sphere operated differently at different sites, with some acting as major suppliers of raw materials, others as manufacturing centers, still others as consumers, and combinations thereof. In other words, regional traditions with different adaptations to local environments, different utilitarian artifacts for exploiting these environments, and different artifact styles were linked by the exchange of status materials among the elites of these various regions. As Struever and Houart (1972, p. 49) point out, "certain items may have functioned to communicate status, while others served as paraphenalia in the ritual reinforcement of status." By separating the function of status goods from common ones, archaeologists were able to reject the older view of a homogeneous Hopewell culture.

In summary, the early archaeological speculation about a lost race of Moundbuilders with origins in the Old World was able to flourish in the absence of good, reliable archaeological data. As more field research was undertaken and field methods improved, this view lost all currency among professionals. Despite recent attempts to attribute Old World influences to the mound sites, there is strong evidence for a long indigenous sequence of development at the Hopewell sites. The discovery and excavation of many burial mounds containing similar artifacts prompted the naive view of a Hopewell culture that arose in Ohio and spread throughout eastern North America. Archaeologists first assumed this culture to be a homogenous, univariate phenomenon that diffused from a single center. Finally, as archaeological sampling moved beyond the highly visible burial mounds to habitation areas, and as archaeologists began to define a culture as a differentiated, multivariate phenomenon, the concept of a Hopewell interaction sphere emerged.

Thus the simple diffusionist view was replaced by a more complex hypothesis of intricate elite trade and exchange over large distances. As we shall see in our discussion of modern archaeological perspectives on Stonehenge, diffusion as a major explanatory device is rarely sufficient by itself. Many pseudoscientific writers assume diffusion over large distances to be a self-contained explanation divorced from examinations of the recipient and donor cultures, but modern archaeologists have broadened their emphasis from exclusive considerations of where new materials and ideas come from (whether foreign or local) to include as well considerations of why and how they are accepted and integrated by some cultures and rejected by others. Studies of the nature of innovation and its adaptive role have also contributed to this new archaeological perspective.

We cannot now say that the concept of an interaction sphere and a systems view are definitely correct. However, the idea of looking at the functions of different cultural subsystems in the context of general questions of how and why cultures develop over time now appears to be a more productive approach to the past than the traditional normative view, and the results it has produced so far seem to better fit our current knowledge of the archaeological record. With more excavation and sophisticated artifact analysis as well as newer research strategies, an even better understanding of eastern North American sites between 100 BC and AD 600 may emerge in the future.

We of course would like to conclude that the current archaeological theories are correct, but we must leave open the possibility that future research will provide us with a new perspective. Unlike many pseudoscientific writers, archaeologists hesitate to speak in terms of right or wrong but, as Bruce Trigger (1978, p. 17) has said, tend to speak of "not-so-good and better." This characteristic of caution in drawing conclusions from archaeological data is one of the chief differences between scientific archaeology and pseudoarchaeology.

Archaeologists are explicitly concerned with the scientific testing of hypotheses about cultural processes. If pseudoscientific writers need to learn more about cultural relativism and published archaeological data, as well as recent developments in the discipline of archaeology, they also need to gain a better understanding of the scientific method. Adherence to the basic tenets of the scientific method is the main criterion for distinguishing between archaeology and pseudoarchaeology.

A recent book by Charles J. Cazeau and Stuart D. Scott, entitled *Exploring the Unknown*, and an incisive article by John R. Cole, "Cult Archaeology and Unscientific Method and Theory," provide excellent analyses of the unscientific nature of most pseudoscientific presentations. Cole considers a basic characteristic of pseudoarchaeologists to be their "atheoretical particularism"; that is, they ignore the "distinction between assertion and theory, being content with particulars out of context" (1980, p. 6).

Such atheoretical procedures are unacceptable to professional archaeologists. Most archaeologists today would agree that any research strategy should clarify and make explicit all assumptions, should carefully and explicitly formulate hypotheses and relate them to previous work, should plan adequate tests for these hypotheses, and should specify a methodology for obtaining needed data for the tests. Relevant research and analysis are then undertaken. The results of such research will subsequently lead to support for or rejection of the hypotheses. In many cases, the research will lead to a reformulation of the hypotheses, more sophisticated methodologies, better tests, and so on, in an ongoing process.

Interested readers and the popular media should expect and require some degree of scientific rigor in the presentations of hypotheses about archaeological phenomena. Unfortunately, one of the prices we must pay for the privilege of sharing a free marketplace of ideas is the possibility that some writers will write unfounded speculations, some publishers will publish them, some bookstores will sell them, and some media will sensationalize them. In this way, unfounded speculations become widely spread among the general population of interested readers. Perhaps the best solution to this problem is to help readers to become aware of the standards of scientific research so that scientific approaches can be better appreciated and pseudoscientific approaches can be read critically.

Let us now turn to several ancient archaeological phenomena—Stonehenge, the pyramids of Egypt and Mesoamerica, and the Nazca lines—that have attracted professional and popular interest. The introductory remarks that follow provide a broad archaeological context for the articles reprinted in this book. In particular, my summaries of current archaeological thought about these phenomena show how such thinking has been supported (or can be tested) by available data, in contrast to pseudoarchaeological views that are less plausible or untestable. The reading list at the end of this Introduction will guide the reader in further exploring contemporary archaeological writings on Stonehenge, the ancient Egyptian and Mesoamerican pyramids, and the Nazca lines.

STONEHENGE

> It was natural that Stonehenge should attract early and hold consistently the attention of antiquaries and prehistorians. It is far and away the most impressive prehistoric monument north of the Great Pyramids. And, like the Pyramid of Cheops, it has been the subject of innumerable esoteric and mystical theories and cults that are still—in the teeth of all scientific evidence—very much alive.
>
> Geoffrey Bibby

An incredible number of words, enlightening and useless alike, have been written about Stonehenge, the great structure on the Salisbury Plain of England. To someone like myself, who has excavated at ancient Maya ruins, Stonehenge is not impressive in size. Yet its stark simplicity and its dominance of the landscape have astounded viewers and attracted interest for centuries.

Until modern excavations revealed Stonehenge's structural sequence and cultural associations, the field was open for all manner of speculation about Stonehenge and other stone circles. As James Fergusson noted in 1872 (in *Rude Stone Monuments in All Countries*, p. vi),

> Till antiquaries are agreed whether the circles are temples or tombs or observatories. . .it seems impossible, without arguing every point, to write anything that will be generally accepted. Still more, till it is decided whether they are really prehistoric or were erected at the periods where tradition and history place them, it seems vain to attempt to explain in a simple narrative form either their age or uses.

Among the favorite candidates for the builders of Stonehenge have been Merlin (of King Arthur's day), Romans, Danes, Egyptians, and Druids. Merlin was suggested as early as the twelfth century AD by Geoffrey of Monmouth, while attribution to the Druids had its inception in the seventeenth century in the writings of John Aubrey. Aubrey's suggestions were then picked up and popularized even further in the following century by William Stukeley.

All these speculations were slowly put to rest, at least as far as professional archaeologists were concerned, as archaeological knowledge about Stonehenge and its region began to increase in both quantity and quality. In particular, by the mid part of this century, archaeological researchers such as Richard Atkinson, Stuart Piggott, and J. F. S. Stone had elucidated the sequence of construction of Stonehenge, obtained cultural associations for the different construction periods, determined the first absolute dates for Stonehenge through the radiocarbon method of dating, and begun to clarify its position in the late Neolithic and early Bronze Age cultures of British prehistory. With the publication of Atkinson's *Stonehenge* in 1956, the archaeology of this great monument had come of age, although some individuals, such as modern-day Druids or certain pseudoarchaeological writers, continue to speculate about Stonehenge.

Jacquetta Hawkes' article "Stonehenge," first published in *Scientific American* in 1953 and reprinted here (p. 39), gives a clear overview of our knowledge about Stonehenge. She discusses the layout of the site, its basic cultural sequence and dating, and the sources of its exotic stones. The archaeological

study of Stonehenge has, of course, continued since the 1950s. The past quarter-century has witnessed significant advances in our understanding of the monument, principally in two areas of research, the dating of Stonehenge and the interpretation of the astronomical function of the monument.

The invention of radiocarbon, or carbon-14, dating by Willard F. Libby in 1949 enabled archaeologists for the first time to assign absolute dates to many of their sequences. As Hawkes indicates, by the early 1950s archaeologists had placed the initial construction of Stonehenge at around 2000 BC and its height at after 1800 BC. These dates immediately enabled archaeologists to reject some of the traditional speculations about the builders of Stonehenge, while cultural associations eliminated others. For example, a date of 1800 BC clearly eliminates the possibility that Romans or Druids built the monument. As regards the latter, Atkinson (1956, p. 179) emphatically states that "there is *no* evidence for connecting the Druids with Stonehenge in any way whatsoever."

However, scientists soon came to realize that some of Libby's original assumptions about carbon-14 dating had to be modified and that a new calibration system for carbon-14 dates was needed. As Colin Renfrew discusses in his *Scientific American* article "Carbon 14 and the Prehistory of Europe" (p. 47), scientists discovered that preliminary datings were off, depending on the time period, by a few years or by a number of centuries. Using samples of old bristle-cone pine trees, which were dated by their tree rings, scientists have been able to work out a correction factor for carbon-14 dates from varying time periods.

As Renfrew forcefully argues, the newly calibrated carbon-14 dates, some of which turn out to far precede the original estimates, have caused archaeologists to revise their thinking about ancient cultural developments in several areas. Such revisions have had great effect on hypotheses about Western Europe in general and about Stonehenge in particular. Until recently, many archaeologists believed that the stimulus and model for various complex developments in Western Europe during the second millennium BC originated in the central Mediterranean, and the preliminary dating supported the view. For instance, in discussing the nature of the Wessex culture in Britain and its trade with other continental groups, Atkinson (1956, pp. 163–164) queries:

> And yet were these Wessex chieftains *alone* responsible for the design and construction of this last and greatest monument at Stonehenge? . . . It seems to me that to account for these exotic and unparallelled features one *must* assume the existence of influence from the only contemporary European cultures in which *architecture*, as distinct from mere construction, was already a living tradition; that is from the Mycenaean and Minoan civilizations of the central Mediterranean. . . . Is it then any more incredible that the architect of Stonehenge should himself have been a Mycenaean, than that the monument should have been designed and erected, with all its unique and sophisticated detail, by mere barbarians?

In other words, many archaeologists thought that ideas and people diffused from the Mediterranean region to Western Europe and influenced the local cultures.

But when the carbon-14 dates for Stonehenge and other sites in Britain and on the Continent were corrected according to the new figures derived from the bristle-cone pine dates, the construction of Stonehenge was found to have preceded the Mycenaean civilization of the central Mediterranean. Dates for the latter had been determined by historical means and were not revised. Thus the new dates indicated that Stonehenge was not derived from Mycenaean civilization but probably was an indigenous development, although the peoples who built the monument during its successive construction periods certainly were in contact with other cultures throughout Europe. As Renfrew concludes, earlier archaeologists had undervalued the originality of the inhabitants of prehistoric Europe and wrongly overestimated the effect of diffusion from the Near East.

An admirable publication of the Royal Commission on Historical Monuments (England) entitled *Stonehenge and Its Environs* summarizes the work of Atkinson and his colleagues at Stonehenge, as discussed by Atkinson in his book *Stonehenge*, along with the corrected carbon-14 dates for the site and some very recent archaeological work. Atkinson defines four basic periods of construction and occupation at Stonehenge (see diagram in Hawkes' article on p. 44 for the location of the various features at Stonehenge). In Period I, which dates from approximately 2800 to 2200 BC (late Neolithic), the ditch and bank were dug and built with one entrance, the Heel Stone was placed in position, and the 56 Aubrey Holes were dug (and soon thereafter refilled). At a later date, some were filled with cremations. As many writers have commented, the site would have been quite unspectacular at this time. In Period II, which dates from approximately 2200 to 2045 BC (the time of Beaker pottery), the four Station Stones were set up (although they might date to the end of Period I), the entrance was widened, the Avenue leading up to the monument was built, and the double circle of bluestones (dolerite from the Preseley Mountains in Southwest Wales) was erected. In Period III, which dates from about 2045 to 1550 BC (Bronze Age, Wessex Culture) and marks the height of Stonehenge, particularly toward the beginning of the period, the Sarsen stones, the heaviest of which weigh 50 tons, were erected in a ring of 30 uprights. Within this ring, a horseshoe of five trilithons with lintels was set up. Later, about 20 bluestones were set up in an oval form, and the Y and Z Holes were excavated. In Period IV, probably around 75 BC, the Avenue was extended to the River Avon.

The second major change in archaeological thinking about Stonehenge also relates to assumptions about the originality and the creativity of the local inhabitants. Within the past two decades, there has been much research and writing about the astronomical aspects of Stonehenge and the intellectual abilities of its builders. Impassioned debate on the possible astronomical functions of Stonehenge and other stone circles in Britain has been in part stimulated by astronomer Gerald Hawkins' research and publications, particularly his book *Stonehenge Decoded*. Although there was a rich tradition of astronomical speculation about Stonehenge prior to the 1960s and some field research (see, for example, Sir Norman Lockyer's *Stonehenge and Other British Stone Monuments Astronomically Considered*, 1906), Hawkins' work caught the attention of both the general public and professional scholars in a way that none of the earlier research had.

Basically, Hawkins argued that Period I Stonehenge had 24 significant alignments that were related to solar and lunar events, such as the summer solstice. He also contended that the Sarsen Stones of Period III Stonehenge had significant alignments and that the 56 Aubrey Holes were used to predict certain lunar eclipses.

The astronomical studies of such scholars as Fred Hoyle, C. A. Newham, and A. S. Thom have also influenced the ongoing debate on Stonehenge's astronomical importance. Even a brief perusal of the pages of the popular British journal *Antiquity* over the past two decades will give the interested reader an appreciation of the flavor of the discussions about Stonehenge and the nature of the disagreements.

As a result of the debate, many scholars would agree with the assessment of astronomer E. C. Krupp (1979, p. 129):

> By this stage we need no longer doubt whether Stonehenge had astronomical significance. Instead, we might marvel that it had so much significance. Its builders and users were capable of remarkable achievements through their own tenacity and their strongly practical and observational approach. It only remains for us to equal their genius and deduce what the deuce they did.

However, while virtually no archaeologist or astronomer would now deny that Stonehenge had some astronomical significance, especially its summer solstice alignment, there are varied opinions about just how much significance it had. Such scholars as Hawkins and Thom believe that the builders of Stonehenge were interested in carefully tracking the movements of the sun and moon. Their view is supported by such archaeologists as Euan MacKie, who views Stonehenge as a great temple and observatory and sees late Neolithic Britain populated by a "hierarchical, stratified society" comparable to that of the Classic Maya in Mesoamerica. MacKie states (1977, pp. 1–2):

> It is hard to believe that there was not at that time a learned and skilled professional order of wise men—perhaps already very old—whose members were able to pursue their studies full time while supported by rural populations, and could command the labour required to erect the hundreds of henge monuments, stone circles and standing stones, some of which were their "observatories."

However, Glyn Daniel, in "Megalithic Monuments" (p. 56), argues that archaeoastronomers have gone overboard in their enthusiasm for finding alignments that indicate ancient interest in the movements of the sun, the moon, and the stars. He also looks askance at claims for great geometrical and measuring skills, such as the use of a regular "megalithic yard," by the builders of Stonehenge. Other scholars have questioned the accuracy of the alignments or have noted that some alignments may be coincidental or not purposeful. The archaeological validity of some claims has also been questioned. In the case of Hoyle's elegant hypothesis about the use of Stonehenge to predict eclipses, some writers such as Krupp feel that, while theoretically possible, the hypothesis demands skills that may have been beyond the knowledge or abilities of the people who built Stonehenge. In addition, such scholars as Aubrey Burl have emphasized that the associations of Stonehenge and stone circles with death ceremonies and perhaps with sorcery may be of greater importance than astronomical functions.

Of course, there are scholars who accept some but not all of the astronomical claims. The arguments of astronomer Owen Gingerich are a good example of such a position. Gingerich's contention, which I find eminently reasonable, accepts Period I (and presumably Period II) Stonehenge as an observatory of the movements of the sun and the moon but does not accept the claims that the Aubrey Holes were used to predict eclipses or eclipse danger periods. He further argues that Period III Stonehenge was not an observatory itself but a monument to the site's earlier uses. He states (1979, p. 117):

> Stonehenge is not so much an ancient megalithic observatory as the *monument to an earlier observatory*. By this I mean that any astronomical sighting lines at Stonehenge must have been well established centuries before they were fossilized into such a heavy, immobile configuration, and the organization of the monumental stones is primarily dictated by the aesthetic symmetry along their principal axis and not by a secondary series of lunar sightlines, as some have proposed. At best Stonehenge was a ritual center commemorating by-gone discoveries, not a site where new knowledge of the heavens was actively sought.

Moreover, I believe that neither the considerable intellectual achievements of the buildings of Period I Stonehenge nor the technological accomplishments of the Period III builders required a highly stratified society (on the order of the Classic Maya), for which there is little evidence in third millennium BC Britain.

As to some pseudoscientists' claims that Stonehenge was a storage battery for cosmic rays or a landing place for UFOs, there is no evidence in the archaeological record—aside from an impressionistic view of the form of the monument—that would support any such claims. As is often the case with such pseudoscientific arguments, they are stated in such a way that they can be neither supported nor negated. Thus they do nothing to advance our knowledge about the phenomena being considered. In particular, they do not subsequently lead to new testable theories nor new understandings of previously unexplainable archaeological materials. As Carl Sagan (1980, p. xiv) cogently notes: "The well-meaning contention that all ideas have equal merit seems to me little different from the disastrous contention that no ideas have any merit." In addition, archaeologists have plausibly argued how the erection of the great trilithons of Stonehenge could have been accomplished, given the technology and manpower available to the builders of the site (see Atkinson, 1956). Moreover, anthropologists, most prominently C. J. Erasmus, have convincingly shown that huge labor pools or highly complex political organizations are not required to build large scale monuments. Scholars have also shown how the bluestones could have been brought from Wales and the Sarsens from Marlborough Downs by these builders. One does not need to invoke extraterrestrial influences to explain these movements. Finally, we should dismiss Von Däniken's notion that Stonehenge contains "relics. . .which could be of tremendous importance for the further development of present-day space travel" (1971, p. 94). No such relics have been found under Stonehenge, and there are no indications that any ever will. Thus, although Stonehenge is unique, many of its features are consistent with local cultural developments, and the construction of the monument forms a long, continuous history.

No matter how the debate on the astronomical significance of Stonehenge is resolved, we do know that this great monument went through several stages of construction between 2800 and 1100 BC and that it was a major technological and intellectual achievement of a succession of indigenous British cultures that probably used the site for a variety of astronomical and religious purposes for many centuries. Whether this ritual site was related to the worship of celestial dieties, to burial ceremonies, or other observances, we do not know. In fact, we may never know what its exact function was. However, we are in a position to understand the cultural contexts within which it was constructed and to attempt to uncover the reasons for its development and ultimate demise.

MARKINGS IN THE PERUVIAN DESERT

> The lines were laid down by a non-literate culture, and after successive conquests nothing concerning their beliefs remains in the present-day folklore. We are separated by an immense gulf of cognitive perception from this lost culture.
>
> Gerald S. Hawkins

The enigmatic markings in the desert in and near the Nazca Valley of southern Peru have intrigued archaeologists and pseudoarchaeologists alike for many years. These markings are raised earth lines in the form of geometrical and animal and plant figures. Dedicated researchers, most particularly Maria Reiche, have patiently surveyed, mapped, and photographed these markings over several decades. Nevertheless, despite our vastly increased knowledge about these markings, the exact purpose of the markings still remains unclear. Archaeologists are usually unable to offer exact reconstructions of prehistoric phenomena; thus, the Nazca markings are not a unique mystery. However, in many cases, archaeologists can offer contextually plausible and at least partially testable hypotheses about such phenomena. In this regard, Peter White (1976, p. 88) points out that the scholars are currently examining two hypotheses about the Nazca markings. The first is that the ancient peoples used the ground "as a canvas on which to sketch important observations relevant to aspects of religious or everyday life"; the second is that the lines are "a kind of architecture, the monumental record of some ritual activity."

As William Isbell indicates in his *Scientific American* article "The Prehistoric Ground Drawings of Peru" (p. 68), we now know that the markings date from 200 BC to AD 600 and that they were constructed by the people who inhabited the nearby sites and manufactured the distinctive Nazca pottery in the Early Intermediate period. Moreover, Isbell puts forth the plausible general hypothesis that "the ground drawings at Nazca were primarily a product of social mechanisms for regulating the balance between resources and population" and that they served a function analogous to the huge contemporary structures in the Moche Valley on the North Coast of Peru. Nevertheless, although Isbell articulates a reasonable hypothesis for the causes of the Nazca markings, other hypotheses that ostensibly account for the purpose of the markings remain controversial.

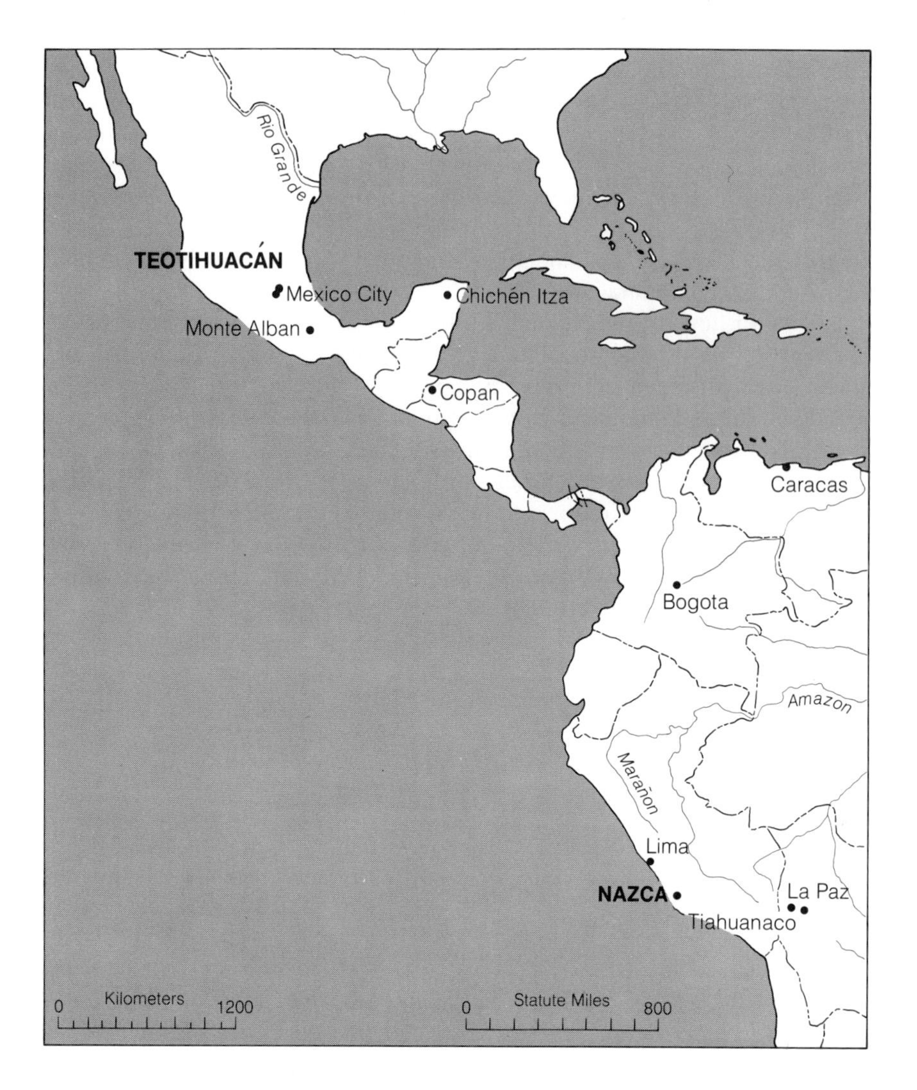

Some of the latter hypotheses clearly are much less likely than others. For example, the hypotheses that the lines might be irrigation canals or roadways were rejected decades ago by Paul Kosok on the grounds of form alone. The workings could not conduct water and do not connect water sources with fields, nor could they conveniently act as walkways; in fact, they criss-cross each other without appearing to lead anywhere. Pauwels and Bergier (1964, p. 117) argued many years ago that "photographs taken of the plain of Nazca remind one irresistably of the ground lighting of an airfield." Erich Von Däniken in *Chariots of the Gods?* argues that the markings are an airfield used for landing vehicles from outer space. Yet there is no direct evidence whatsoever for the presence of extraterrestrial beings on the plains of Nazca. In addition, as several writers have pointed out, Von Däniken's conjecture is extremely ethnocentric. Why should extraterrestrial beings who presumably had sufficiently advanced technology to fly their spaceships through light-years of space need airfields that are similar to those used by our own conventional airplanes? In *Gods from Outer Space*, Von Däniken (1972, p. 105) notes that "at some time in the past, unknown intelligences landed on the uninhabited plain near the present-day town of Nazca and built an improvised airfield for their spacecraft which were to operate in the vicinity of the earth." They then left the earth, according to Von Däniken. The Nazca peoples who saw them longed for their return and made more landing strips and then figures in order to attract the "gods" to return. However, except for the impressionistic argument based on form, there is no archaeological evidence to support this view. As Maria Reiche has pointed out, the technological skills needed to plan and execute the lines and figures were within the capabilities of the peoples who inhabited nearby sites during the Early Intermediate period. Reiche shows how the lines and figures could have been planned and executed from the ground, perhaps using small-scale models, without any help from visitors from outer space. Von Däniken's argument is like a "just-so" story: It is not testable, it does not shed new light on other related data, and it is not less complicated than existing archaeological hypotheses. Von Däniken's conjectures do not advance our understanding of the Nazca lines.

Other writers also have looked to the skies for answers to questions about the Nazca markings, but their hypotheses are not as extreme as Von Däniken's, and they have the merit of being simpler and testable. For example, Paul Kosok entitled a chapter in *Land, Life, and Water in Ancient Peru* on the Nazca markings "The Largest Astronomy Book in the World." He believes that the lines had astronomical significance and that such astronomical knowledge was used for calendrical purposes to predict the coming of water for irrigation. He further speculates that the narrow enclosures formed by the lines might have been used for ceremonial races, while the figures might have been clan totems or symbols of star constellations. Luis Lumbreras (1974) also believes the markings to be part of some ritual relating to agriculture, specifically that they served an astrological purpose in predicting the availability of water. He argues that there are indications of social stratification in the Nazca tombs and that specialists, perhaps priests, utilized the desert markings as a stellar calendar to predict the coming of water for irrigation.

However, Gerald Hawkins, whose research greatly influenced our current understanding of Stonehenge, contends that the Nazca lines do not have astronomical significance. For example, he found that only about one-fifth of the lines (39 of a sample of 186) pointed to important positions of the sun or moon on the horizons. Hawkins (1974, p. 140) states:

> The ancient lines in the desert near Nasca show no preference for the directions of the sun, moon, planets, or brighter stars. Nor do the lines show any deliberate alignment with a fixed but unidentifiable object in the sky, such as a nova or the center of some ancient pattern of stars. Thus, the pattern of lines as a whole cannot be explained as astronomical, nor are they calendric.

Other scholars have disputed Hawkins' findings. Gary Urton, for example, argues that Hawkins' study ignores Andean ethnoastronomy (modern native astronomy) and thus operates under the false assumption that the Nazca lines must point to something on the horizon in order to be significant. Urton (1979, p. 32) asks:

> In most of Andean astronomy, the *zenith* position of a celestial body is as important as the position of its rise or set. This being the case, I propose that an equally valid astronomical question to ask of the Nazca lines and figures is: How will the constellations, and *the lines connecting the stars*, be reflected on the surface of the earth?

William Isbell specifically notes that Hawkins ignores the zenith and nadir sun that were so important to later Peruvian peoples such as the Inca. Isbell, in fact, considers the 39 positive astronomical alignments found by Hawkins to be quite significant and, contrary to Hawkins, feels that this number of alignments supports rather than negates the astronomical hypotheses. He also points out that Hawkins, following his Stonehenge research, looked for important alignments at the opposite ends of the Nazca lines (such as summer and winter positions), whereas opposite directions are not significant at Nazca, given the local mountainous topography (unlike the open plain location of Stonehenge). Isbell also has technical criticisms of the nature of the observations and maps used by Hawkins. Nevertheless, even if one accepts the various criticisms of Hawkins' work, his findings indicate that proponents of the astronomical interpretation of the Nazca lines have much work to do in order to prove their hypotheses.

Another group of scholars, whose work in many ways complements rather than opposes the astronomical hypotheses, have argued that the Nazca markings had ritual or ceremonial significance. In fact, it probably would be impossible to separate the astronomical and ritual aspects of the markings. Paul Kosok, Maria Reiche, and others contend that one of the functions of the markings was to serve as sacred walkways for rituals. This contention would apply to the figures as well as to the lines. Similarly, Alan Sawyer (cited by McIntyre, 1975, p. 725) has noted:

> Most figures are composed of a single line that never crosses itself, perhaps the path of a ritual maze. If so, when the Nazcas walked the line, they could have felt they were absorbing the essence of whatever the drawing symbolized.

Hawkins extends the idea of ritual significance in suggesting that the whole Nazca plain functioned as a sacred place or monument and that the whole area on which the markings were made played a major ritual role in very important prehistoric ceremonies. Clearly, the problem for archaeologists is to design research strategies that will permit them to form testable hypotheses from such speculations about ritual significance.

Many of the speculations that have been advanced to explain the Nazca markings suffer from an ethnocentric bias—that is, they view the Nazca phenomenon from the perspective of the writer's own culture and not necessarily from the perspective of the peoples of the Nazca region. For example, Von Däniken suggests that the lines and figures make sense only if they were intended to be visible to living beings viewing them from the air. But even if the lines and figures were constructed to be viewed from the air, it does not necessarily follow that they were intended for extraterrestrial visitors. A more likely possibility is that the prehistoric inhabitants of the region made the markings generally for the "deities in the heavens" rather than specifically for "gods from outer space."

As many writers have noted, while the quantity and magnitude of the Nazca markings are exceptional, they are not a unique phenomenon. There are many other examples of what has been termed *invisible art*. In Peru itself, some non-Nazca ground markings have been discovered. Moreover, there is good evidence that, subsequent to the time when the Nazca markings were made, other Andean peoples built constructions that were not meant to be viewed from a conventional ground-level perspective. The city of Cuzco, as one example, was built by the Incas in the shape of a puma and had significant astronomical alignments as well. Throughout history, monuments and altars have often been built "for the gods," who were not conceived of as actual living beings from outer space, as Von Däniken and other pseudoarchaeologists would have us believe.

Although we still do not know the ancient purpose or purposes of the Nazca markings, archaeologists have advanced several plausible and potentially testable hypotheses that attempt to account for these markings. As we have seen, these recent hypotheses have their strengths and weaknesses. We have also seen that there is no direct evidence for extraterrestrials at Nazca and no need to invoke them. The Nazca markings can be explained and probably will eventually be explained within the cultural context of Nazca in particular and Andean civilization in general.

PYRAMIDS

> Usually scientists are willing to give any theory, however doubtful, a try, provided it shows imagination and it offers new ideas. When the late Wolfgang Pauli was asked to assess a somewhat unimaginative research paper, he sadly shook his head and said: "It isn't even wrong." However, scientists also know that new ideas are worthless, unless they can be checked and supported by confirmatory evidence. For instance, the notion that the moon is made of green cheese had been made unlikely by a great deal of solid research—even before astronauts went there and established that it is made of rock. It is much the same with the great number of pyramid theories which have been put forward throughout the ages.
>
> Kurt Mendelssohn

> The pyramids have suffered long and hard at the hands of their interpreters, many of whose ponderous hypotheses of the true purpose of the monuments seem to outweigh even the enormous limestone blocks of which the pyramids were built.
>
> E. C. Krupp

Pyramidal architecture of one kind or another can be found in several areas of the world. The pyramids of ancient Egypt, particularly the Great Pyramid of Cheops (Khufu), and ancient Mesoamerica, particularly those found at the urban center of Teotihuacán, have attracted special attention over the years as the most outstanding examples of this type of architecture. The pyramids have been the subject of much pseudoarchaeological speculation as well as scientific research. The recent speculations of Von Däniken and others are just contemporary versions of a long tradition of speculation about such monuments.

In general, the pseudoarchaeological approach to pyramids is quite similar to speculations about other ancient phenomena, although the lengths to which various writers have gone to argue their cases may be more excessive than in other examples. One pseudoscientific approach is to attribute all kinds of purposes to the pyramids that the professional archaeologists have ignored. Unlike those who look askance at the possibility of great achievements by many ancient peoples, proponents of this perspective go to the other extreme in seeing all manner of unlikely ancient achievements. A second and related approach is to further speculate that, given all the amazing purposes of the pyramids, some group other than the native population must have been responsible for their construction. Indeed, the more purposes the proponents of the first approach advance, the more that speculators of the second approach feel encouraged to conjecture that a nonnative population, such as ancient astronauts, were involved in their construction.

Let us turn our attention first to Egypt. An example of the pseudoscientific approaches to the pyramids is that of Pauwels and Bergier (1964, p. 110), who contend that "we know today that the Pharaohs embodied in the Pyramids the findings of a science of whose origins and methods we know nothing." Peter Tompkins, in *Secrets of the Great Pyramid* (1971, p. xiv), states that "the common—and indeed authoritative—assumption that the Pyramid was just another tomb built to memoralize some vainglorious Pharoah is proved to be false." Tompkins further contends that "whoever built the Great Pyramid, it is now quite clear, knew the precise circumference of the planet, and the length of the year to several decimals. . . . Its architects may well have known the mean length of the earth's orbit round the sun, the specific density of the planet, the 26,000-year cycle of the equinoxes, the acceleration of gravity, and the speed of light" (pp. xiv–xv), as well as other esoteric information. But as numerous scholars—including Peter White, E. C. Krupp, Clif-

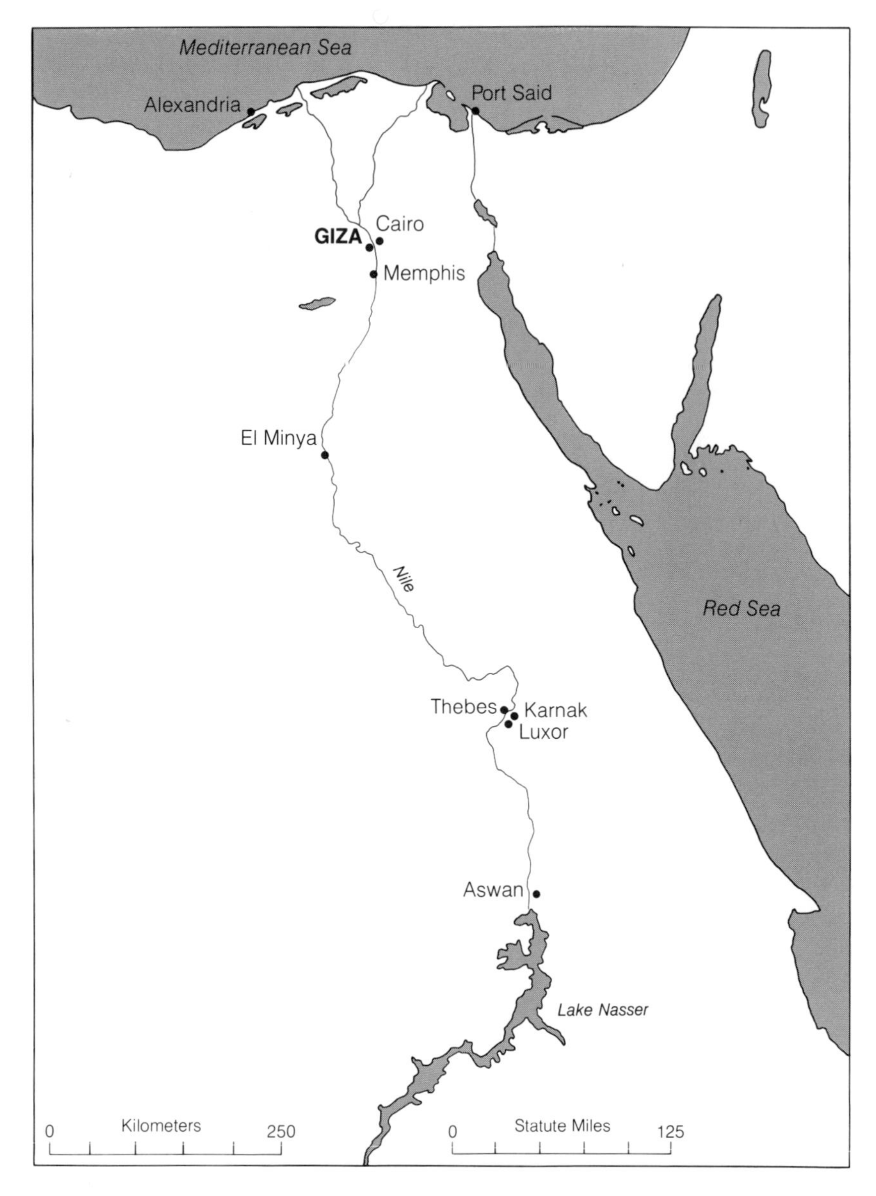

ford Wilson, and Willy Ley—have noted, arguments that designers of the Great Pyramid (built by the Pharaoh Cheops during his reign from 2638–2613 BC) had such esoteric knowledge by and large are not supported by critical comparisons with known data. Many of the ideas discussed by Tompkins have been current for years. Charles Piazzi Smyth's *Our Inheritance in the Great Pyramid*, published in 1890, was particularly influential in stimulating speculations about esoteric knowledge hidden in the dimensions of the Great Pyramid. However, as our knowledge has grown about this monument in particular and Egyptian archaeology in general, we have found that the data fail to support Smyth's argument.

Many of the claims for hidden knowledge in the Great Pyramid are based on inaccurate or inexact measurements. Because most of the pyramid's outer facing is gone, totally accurate measurements are impossible. For example, many years ago, Flinders Petrie showed that Charles Piazzi Smyth's contention that the ancient Egyptians used a standard measurement (which he terms the *pyramid inch*) was unfounded because it was based on inaccurate measurements. For another example, the claim that the height of the Great Pyramid is related to the weight of our planet is not supportable, because the best available measurements of the height of the monument simply are not mathematically related to the weight of the Earth. As archaeologist Peter White notes, anyone can play games with numbers. He points out that the height of the Eiffel Tower multiplied by a million and converted to a speed measurement is virtually the same figure as the speed of light. In the case of the Eiffel Tower, we know that the similarity of figures is pure coincidence. Since such numerical coincidences are possible, even likely, in comparisons of architectural measurements with modern scientific knowledge, we must be very cautious in attributing modern knowledge to the ancient builders of monuments.

Another persistent claim about the Great Pyramid is that its measurements indicate that its builders knew about pi (π). However, scholars such as Peter White and Willy Ley argue that there is no concrete evidence that the ancient Egyptians used the sophisticated mathematical concept of pi. Rather, they may have used the geometrically derived ratio of 22/7, which approximates pi. This ratio probably was derived from the Egyptian measuring system of palms, ells, and other units (about which we have a reasonable amount of information from ancient writings and modern analyses by scholars such as Ludwig Borchardt). For example, for a number of pyramids, the height multiplied by 22/7 equals the sum of the length of two of the sides at the base. As Ley (1969) argues, the individuals who supervised the construction of the pyramids probably "carried, in the last stages of the building, the triangles made for a slope of $5\frac{1}{2}$ palms per ell of vertical height, the proportion which was destined to cause so much confusion thousands of years later."

There does appear to be support for some of the claims for astronomical orientations for the pyramids. In relation to the Great Pyramid, for example, astronomer E. C. Krupp (1976b, p. 236) points out that "although it seems certain that the Great Pyramid was astronomically oriented, its use as an observatory is unsupported." It also appears likely that the two shafts that lead from the King's chamber to the outside walls of the pyramid have stellar orientations. These shafts have often been called ventilation shafts, but ventilation probably was not their main function. Rather, as Krupp notes, astronomer Virginia Trimble and archaeologist Alexander Badawy argue that these shafts may have been built to allow the Pharaoh Cheops to rise to the stars through the passages. At the time of Cheops, one shaft was aligned with the star Thuban in the constellation Draco (the Dragon), and the second was aligned with Orion's belt, which was associated with Osiris, according to Egyptian beliefs.

Among other views of the pyramids, we have Von Däniken's assertion that the Egyptians did not have the technical knowledge, support base, or manpower to build the huge pyramids of the Fourth and Fifth Dynasties of the Old Kingdom (of the middle third millennium BC). He states (1971, p. 74) that "if we meekly accept the neat package of knowledge that the Egyptologists serve up to us, ancient Egypt appears suddenly and without transition with a fantastic and ready-made civilization." However, Von Däniken simply ignores all the evidence for the long development of society in ancient Egypt, which provided the foundations on which the achievements of the Fourth Dynasty rested. As Ronald Story (1977, p. 61) rightfully asks: "Is he [Von Däniken] serious? If he had looked at almost any *one* of the approximately twenty thousand volumes of books and periodicals that have been written on the subject, he would have realized the absurdity of such a statement." Walter B. Emery's *Scientific American* article "The Tombs of the First Pharaohs" (p. 78) describes the funerary antecedents to the pyramids; he then notes some of the continuities from the First and Second Dynasties to the Third through Fifth Dynasties of the Old Kingdom. Although Emery, writing in 1957, points to the possibilities of influences from neighboring groups on the early growth of Egyptian civilization, many archaeologists today seem to view this development as essentially an indigenous one. But even the view that neighboring groups influenced the development of early Egyptian culture counters Von Däniken's assertion that Egyptologists posit the sudden appearance of a sophisticated Egyptian civilization.

As various scholars point out, there is an evolution in the form of Egyptian funerary monuments that culminates in the use of the pyramid in the Fourth Dynasty. I. E. S. Edwards describes in his excellent book *The Pyramids of Egypt* the historical construction sequence from *mastabas* (tombs covered by rectangular structures) to step pyramids to true pyramids. He suggests that the latter two forms may have had direct religious relevance, with the step form allowing the dead Pharaoh to climb to the sky and the true pyramid symbolizing the rays of the sun spreading out from the heavens. The change from one form to the other may have reflected a shift in religious emphasis or beliefs. Recently, the scholar Farouk El-Baz (1981) has argued that the inspiration for the pyramidal form may have been its superior resistance to wind erosion. Moreover, the pyramid form could have been observed by the ancient Egyptians in natural desert land forms.

Although the forms and the beliefs may have evolved, the principal function of the monuments definitely was to serve as tombs for the rulers of ancient Egypt and to glorify their status and power. Moreover, the internal form of the monuments, the decorations, and the contents of internal chambers and associated structures were all constructed in a manner that would allow the Pharaoh to continue to function in his customary manner in the afterlife.

Although the ostensible reasons for the building of the pyramids are clear, the underlying cultural reasons are not as obvious. Since many archaeologists see explanation as a major goal of their research, they consistently try to place the function of various traits, such as monuments, in larger cultural contexts. As difficult as historical reconstruction is, even when such efforts are aided by written documents (as is the case in the study of ancient Egypt), the development of theory is often even more difficult. Nevertheless, for the professional archeologist, description and theory-building must go hand in hand.

A recent and particularly interesting attempt to place the achievements of the Old Kingdom in context has been made by Karl Butzer, a geologist and archaeologist. Butzer discerns several systemically reinforcing factors, including the amount of flooding by the Nile, population level, and agricultural techniques, as relating to the nature of political development. He notes a correlation between the decline in the flow of the Nile and population decline. He further points out that the rise of the Third Dynasty (around 2760 BC), which ushered in the great age of pyramid building of the Third to Fifth Dynasties, was preceded by an era, the Second Dynasty (2970–2760 BC), of "political instability, revolts, reduced foreign trade, and probable impoverishment. Nile floods declined by an overall 30 percent, and in some years failed entirely" (1980, p. 519). The increase in the average discharge of the Nile in the Third Dynasty, the better floods, and increased agricultural production provided the ecological base for the achievements of the Old Kingdom. The improved environmental conditions and consequent rise in population supplied the Pharaohs with the means to undertake major building projects, namely, manpower and the resources to support the workers.

Kurt Mendelssohn, a physicist and amateur Egyptologist, argues in *The Riddle of the Pyramids* that the building of the huge labor-intensive monuments of the Fourth Dynasty in particular enabled the Pharaohs to strengthen their political hold on the Egyptian people. Egypt had been unified for only a relatively short period of time before the onset of pyramid building. In Mendelssohn's words, "the pyramids were more important than the pharaohs whose names they immortalize" (1971, p. 220). He argues that monumental construction was a continuous activity and that more than one pyramid might have been under construction at a time. Such a procedure would have allowed the rulers to use the huge workforce needed to construct the pyramids efficiently year after year without long interruptions. Arguing along

The Pyramid of the Sun at the ancient Mexican city of Teotihuacán.

the same lines as William Isbell does with the Nazca data, Mendelssohn also points out that the huge building activities came early in the history of Egypt because they served to consolidate and strengthen centralized authority and control. Although specific aspects of Mendelssohn's detailed hypothesis may prove wrong, his overall argument—that the pyramids served not only as tombs and religious sites but also symbolized for the Egyptians the immense power and importance of their rulers and served as the means by which that power was consolidated—is compelling.

The immense Pyramid of the Sun at the vast Pre-Columbian urban center of Teotihuacán in the Basin of Mexico (just to the northeast of modern-day Mexico City) also was built early in the history of the city, well before its full development. Mendelssohn, in fact, argues that his theory works for ancient Mexico and particularly Teotihuacán as well as for Egypt. As René Millon, who has spent years studying this great Mexican center, describes in his *Scientific American* article "Teotihuacán" (p. 85), the city began to grow two centuries before the time of Christ. By the middle of the first millennium AD, Teotihuacán's population may have reached 200,000, while the city spread over 20 square kilometers; it became the preeminent political and economic power in Mesoamerica. The Pyramid of the Sun was built by AD 150–200; the Pyramid of the Moon was built somewhat later. It should be noted that the names for these structures were later inventions and probably not the names used by the ancient Teotihuacanos.

The Pyramids of the Sun and the Moon, like other Mesoamerican pyramids, are not true pyramids but rather are truncated step-structures that supported temples on their tops. Although some of the pyramids contained large tombs, as in Egypt, most served solely as bases for temples. Probably the largest number of Mesoamerican pyramids can be found in the Maya area; these structures were built for nearly 2000 years, until the time of the Spanish Conquest (AD 1519).

The Pyramid of the Sun at Teotihuacán is perhaps the best known of the Mesoamerican pyramids. Its basal measurements are very close to those of the Pyramid of Cheops, but it is not nearly as tall. Recent discoveries indicate that it was built over a cave that almost certainly functioned as a shrine. In other words, the location of the pyramid probably had religious significance. The massiveness of the structure and the whole Street of the Dead upon which it is situated clearly were intended to impress visitors to the city. As Millon (1976, p. 226) notes, "when one has walked the 'Street of the Dead'. . .it is difficult to avoid the conclusion that one of the purposes its architects had in mind was to overwhelm the viewer, to impress upon him the power and glory of the gods of Teotihuacán and their earthly representatives."

The rapid growth of Teotihuacán probably was due to the interaction of several major factors, including its access to an important obsidian resource, the potential for intensive irrigation agriculture in the Teotihuacán Valley, and the natural trade routes to the east and south that would have passed through the valley. Soon after a volcanic eruption occasioned the demise of one of its principal rivals, the city of Cuicuilco, Teotihuacán began to increase dramatically in population, size, and politicoeconomic importance. Of course, the religious significance of the site cannot be overlooked in any examination of the reasons for the growth of Teotihuacán. Some scholars view the building of the Pyramid of the Sun as a means of gaining the allegiance of the growing population of the city to the deities of the state, of symbolizing the state's power and authority, and of attracting immigrants and merchants to the burgeoning city by its size, impressiveness, and religious importance.

Like the Great Pyramid of Cheops, the Pyramid of the Sun and other Mesoamerican temple pyramids have been conjectured to be the repositories of all kinds of esoteric knowledge. Current archaeological data do not support such claims, with one class of exceptions, although it is possible that future research might uncover new data. The class of exceptions pertains to the realm of astronomy. The ancient Mesoamerican peoples were skilled astronomers, and their astronomical knowledge was inextricably entwined with their religious beliefs. The latter pervaded all aspects of life, including, of course, architecture. The Pyramid of the Sun, like the entire city of Teotihuacán, was oriented approximately 15.5° east of north. Various writers have seen solar or stellar significance in this orientation. For example, the highly respected archaeoastronomer Anthony Aveni and other scholars have argued that the orientation may be related to observations of the constellation of the Pleiades, which sets within one degree of the east–west axis of Teotihuacán at the time the city's grid pattern was first formed. Aveni notes that the Pleiades may have held particular significance for the ancient Teotihuacanos because this constellation of stars "underwent heliacal rising on the same day as the first of the two annual passages of the sun across the zenith, a day of great importance in demarcating the seasons" (1979, p. 179).

Aveni's hypothesis is a plausible one and deserves further testing. It is strengthened by two other findings. First, the orientation of structures in central Mexico appears to shift through time in a direction in keeping with Aveni's argument. Second, there are a couple of ring-and-cross designs pecked onto stone at and near the site. The designs may well have been surveying or sighting marks, and they are oriented toward the setting of the Pleiades.

In summary, the pyramids of Egypt and Mexico were great engineering triumphs of the ancient world. Their construction was within the competence of the local population, and as is the case with Stonehenge, there is no good reason to believe that they were not built by local inhabitants. There is no strong evidence to support claims that the pyramids are repositories of vast realms of hidden knowledge, although there are sufficient data to support arguments that they had astronomical significance. The pyramids of Egypt and Mesoamerica had religious importance, the former as tombs for the Pharaohs, the latter as bases for temples (although some also housed tombs). Their construction involved labor-intensive efforts that probably aided elite groups in strengthening their power over the populace and served as symbols of their new authority. Finally, there is no evidence to support the argument that there were direct connections between the ancient Egyptians (who built the Great Pyramid between 2638 and 2613 BC) and the Mexicans (who built the Pyramid of the Sun between AD 150 and 200). As Mendelssohn (1974, p. 211) has cogently pointed out, it would have been curious indeed that "the Egyptians should have instructed the Indians in the building of large pyramids, an occupation which they themselves had given up 2000 years earlier."

CONCLUDING REMARKS

It is obvious that pseudoscience in general and pseudoarchaeology in particular are enjoying an immense popularity today. One need only peruse the displays at airport or shopping mall bookstores or turn on a television set to realize that the general public seems to have an insatiable thirst for books and shows about ancient astronauts or pyramid power. In response to this trend, professional archaeologists are writing articles and books devoted to analyses of why people seem to be excited by what most professionals perceive to be crackpot ideas. A number of hypotheses have been brought forward to explain the current surge of interest in pseudoarchaeological presentations. A popular hypothesis is that belief in ancient astronauts and the like serves as a substitute for more orthodox religious beliefs at a time of growing social alienation. This hypothesis has been put forward in several forms and may well have some validity. Or, the explanation may simply be an intrinsic public interest in archaeological or antiquarian pursuits. As Gordon Willey (1980, p. 2) has noted in addrcssing the question of why archaeology attracts such a large number of extravagant claims,

> My best guess about this is that it is because almost everyone is curious about the past. In one way or another, we want the past to be pertinent to the present, to explain it, to justify it. And I think that this means that archaeology will always have a large body of outer adherents, no matter how ulterior their motives may seem, no matter how undisciplined they behave.

Whatever the answer, and I do not have any new insights to offer in this regard, it is clear that pseudoarchaeology is not a new development; its popularity is not necessarily any greater today than it was, say, 150 years ago. The placing of Merlin or the Druids at Stonehenge and the quest for the lost race of Moundbuilders are just two examples of undisciplined speculation in the previous century. In fact, one might well argue that, in terms of the percentage of the population, there was more popular interest in unfounded speculations about lost races in the early nineteenth century United States than there is in ancient astronauts in the United States today. Given that wild speculations have had great appeal for centuries, perhaps our modern mass media simply give pseudoarchaeological conjectures more currency and greater visibility than ever before. Be that as it may, it appears that such speculation will continue to flourish in some form or another. Thus, we should ask not only why pseudoarchaeology flourishes but also how professional archaeologists can effectively counter pseudoarchaeological speculations.

A growing number of archaeologists seem to agree that pseudoarchaeology cannot and should not be ignored. Although the archaeological profession, like many other professional disciplines, has a tradition of ignoring or taking lightly the efforts of professionals who write articles or books for the general public, the recent trend seems to be that professionals increasingly favor efforts to communicate scientific information to the public. To communicate effectively with a popular audience, archaeologists first must present their data in forms that are accessible to the nonprofessional reader. Second, archaeologists should not shy away from rebutting pseudoscientific claims.

The absence of rigorous scientific opposition to pseudoscientific claims may mislead the public to believe that such claims have the scientific community's tacit approval. Third, archaeologists must educate the public about the real nature of their discipline.

In many ways, this third point has been most neglected by the profession. The public seems to have a vast misconception about how archaeologists approach the past. Many people who say they are interested in archaeology seem to lack a basic appreciation of the nature of professional archaeological research. Although very few people would think that they could be physicists without any formal training, many seem to believe that they can be archaeologists without any preparation. This misapprehension is due in large part, I believe, to the failure of professional archaeologists to inform the public about the complexities of undertaking archaeological research and analysis and the rigors of archaeological training. If the public largely views archaeologists as treasure seekers, then the idea that anyone can go out and dig on weekends as well as any archaeologist can becomes more understandable, as does the assumption that any pseudoscientific argument is as strong and as plausible as any professional one.

It is the responsibility of archaeologists to correct the misinformed perspectives on the discipline of archaeology that many members of the popular media and the general public seem to have. *Scientific American* has played an important role in attempting to present significant archaeological findings and ideas to the interested public. I hope that this short book contributes to this crucial effort to present scientific information.

Finally, an important lesson that the history of archaeology teaches us is that a cross-cultural anthropological perspective allows us to appreciate the incredible variety of human achievements throughout history. To return to a point I made at the beginning of this Introduction, when I read or hear someone question how the Maya could have developed hieroglyphic writing without help from others, I respond by referring to the long sequence of development of writing in Mesoamerica prior to the Classic period, the indigeneous development of Maya culture in the jungle lowlands of southern Mesoamerica, and the richness of their other cultural achievements. I can also look at the great cultural achievements of other groups at a comparable level of development—say, in the Near East. The Maya may have been influenced by neighboring groups, but the general development of their culture and the specific achievement of hieroglyphic writing (as well as pyramid building) were well within their capabilities. We need not resort to unprovable, unsubstantiated, and ultimately untestable claims about visits from outer space to understand their achievements or their culture.

SUGGESTED READINGS

Readers may wish to consult the following works from the archaeological and pseudoarchaeological literature. The original bibliographies for the articles appear at the end of this book.

Atkinson, R. J. C. 1956. *Stonehenge*. London: Hamish Hamilton.

Atkinson, R. J. C. 1980. *The Prehistoric Temples of Stonehenge and Avebury*. London: Pitkin Pictorials.

Aveni, Anthony F. 1979. "Astronomy in Ancient Mesoamerica." In *In Search of Ancient Astronomies*, ed. E. C. Krupp. New York: McGraw-Hill, 165–202.

Baity, Elizabeth Chesley. 1973. "Archaeoastronomy and Ethnoastronomy So Far." *Current Anthropology* 14: 389–449.

Bibby, Geoffrey. 1956. *The Testimony of the Spade*. New York: Knopf.

Brose, David S., and N'omi Greber, eds. 1979. *Hopewell Archaeology: The Chillicothe Conference*. Kent, Ohio: Kent State University Press.

Burl, Aubrey. 1979. *Prehistoric Avebury*. New Haven: Yale University Press.

Burl, Aubrey. 1980. "Science or Symbolism: Problems of Archaeo-astronomy." *Antiquity* 54: 191–200.

Butzer, Karl W. 1976. *Early Hydraulic Civilization in Egypt*. Chicago: University of Chicago Press.
Butzer, Karl W. 1980. "Civilizations: Organisms or Systems." *American Scientist* 68: 517–523.
Caldwell, Joseph R. 1964. "Interaction Spheres in Prehistory." In *Hopewellian Studies*, eds. J. R. Caldwell and R. L. Hall. Illinois State Museum Scientific Papers 12, 133–143.
Cazeau, Charles J., and Stuart D. Scott, Jr. 1979. *Exploring the Unknown: Great Mysteries Reexamined*. New York: Plenum.
Cole, John R. 1980. "Cult Archaeology and Unscientific Method and Theory." In *Advances in Archaeological Method and Theory*, vol. 3, ed. Michael B. Schiffer. New York: Academic Press, 1–33.
Daniel, Glyn. 1979. "The Forgotten Milestones and Blind Alleys of the Past." *Royal Anthropological Institute News* 33: 3–6.
Edwards, I. E. S. 1961. *The Pyramids of Egypt*. Harmondsworth, England: Penguin.
El-Baz, Farouk, 1981. "Desert Builders Knew a Good Thing When They Saw It." *Smithsonian* 12 (1): 116–122
Ellegard, Alvar. 1981. "Stone Age Science in Britain?" *Current Anthropology* 22: 99–126.
Erasmus, C. J. 1965. "Monument Building: Some Field Experiments." *Southwestern Journal of Anthropology* 21: 277–301.
Fagan, Brian M. 1981. *In the Beginning*, 4th ed. Boston: Little, Brown.
Fell, Barry. 1976. *America B.C.* New York: Quadrangle Books.
Fergusson, James. 1872. *Rude Stone Monuments in All Countries; Their Age and Uses*. London: John Murray.
Gingerich, Owen. 1979. "The Basic Astronomy of Stonehenge." In *Astronomy of the Ancients*, eds. Kenneth Brecher and Michael Feirtag. Cambridge, Mass.: M.I.T. Press, 117–132.
Hawkins, Gerald S. 1973. *Beyond Stonehenge*. New York: Harper & Row.
Hawkins, Gerald S. 1974. "Prehistoric Desert Markings in Peru." *National Geographic Society Research Reports, 1967*, 117–144.
Hawkins, Gerald S. 1980. "The Need for Objectivity." *Archaeoastronomy* 3 (1): 8–11.
Hawkins, Gerald S., and John B. White. 1965. *Stonehenge Decoded*. Garden City, N.Y.: Doubleday.
Hodson, F. R., ed. 1974. *The Place of Astronomy in the Ancient World*. London: Oxford University Press.
Hoyle, Fred. 1977. *On Stonehenge*. San Francisco: W. H. Freeman and Company.
Isbell, William H. 1979. "Review of *Final Scientific Report for the National Geographic Society Expedition: Ancient Lines* by Gerald S. Hawkins." *Archaeoastronomy* 2 (4): 38–40.
Kosok, Paul. 1965. *Life, Land, and Water in Ancient Peru*. Brooklyn: Long Island University Press.
Kosok, Paul, and Maria Reiche. 1947. "The Mysterious Markings of Nazca." *Natural History* 56 (5): 200–207, 237–238.
Kosok, Paul, and Maria Reiche. 1949. "Ancient Drawings on the Desert of Peru." *Archaeology* 2: 206–215.
Krupp, E. C. 1978. "Great Pyramid Astronomy." *Griffith Observer* 42 (3): 2–18.
Krupp, E. C. 1979a. "The Stonehenge Chronicles." In *In Search of Ancient Astronomies,* ed. E. C. Krupp. New York: McGraw-Hill, 81–132.
Krupp, E. C. 1979b. "Astronomy, Pyramids, and Priests." In *In Search of Ancient Astronomies*, ed. E. C. Krupp. New York: McGraw-Hill, 203–240.
Ley, Willy. 1969. "The Great Pyramid, the Golden Section and Pi." In *Another Look at Atlantis*. Garden City, N.Y.: Doubleday, 27–41.
Lockyer, Norman. 1906. *Stonehenge and Other British Stone Monuments Astronomically Considered*. London: Macmillan.
Lumbreras, Luis G. 1974. *The Peoples and Cultures of Ancient Peru,* trans. Betty J. Meggers. Washington, D.C.: Smithsonian Institution Press.
MacKie, Evan W. 1977. *Science and Society in Prehistoric Britain*. London: Paul Elek.
McIntyre, Loren. 1975. "Mystery of the Nazca Lines." *National Geographic* 7 (5): 716–728.
Megaw, J. V. S., and D. D. A. Simpson. 1979. *Introduction to British Prehistory*. Leicester, England: Leicester University Press.

Mendelssohn, Kurt. 1971. "A Scientist Looks at the Pyramids." *American Scientist* 59: 210–220.

Mendelssohn, Kurt. 1974. *The Riddle of the Pyramids*. New York: Praeger.

Millon, René. 1976. "Social Relations in Ancient Teotihuacán." In *The Valley of Mexico, Studies in Pre-Hispanic Ecology and Society*, ed. Eric R. Wolf. Albuquerque: University of New Mexico Press, 205–248.

Moir, Gordon. 1979. "Hoyle on Stonehenge." *Antiquity* 53: 124–129.

Morrison, Tony. 1978. *Pathways to the Gods: The Mystery of the Andes Lines*. New York: Harper & Row.

Newham, C. A. 1972. *The Astronomical Significance of Stonehenge*. Leeds, England: John Blackburn.

Pauwels, Louis, and Jacques Bergier. 1964. *The Morning of the Magicians*. New York: Stein & Day.

Rathje, William. 1978. "The Ancient Astronaut Myth." *Archaeology* 31: 4–7.

Redman, Charles L., ed. 1973. *Research and Theory in Current Archaeology*. New York: Wiley.

Reiche, Maria. 1968. *Mystery on the Desert*. Stuttgart, Germany: Heinrich Fink.

Renfrew, Colin. 1979. *Before Civilization: The Radiocarbon Revolution and Prehistoric Europe*, new ed. Cambridge, England: Cambridge University Press.

Riley, Carroll L., J. Charles Kelley, Campbell W. Pennington, and Robert L. Rands, eds. 1971. *Man Across the Sea*. Austin: University of Texas Press.

Royal Commission on Historial Monuments (England). 1979. *Stonehenge and Its Environs*. Edinburgh, Scotland: Edinburgh University Press.

Sagan, Carl. 1980. *Broca's Brain*. New York: Ballantine Books.

Shetrone, Henry C. 1920. "The Culture Problem in Ohio Archaeology." *American Anthropologist* 22: 144–172.

Silverberg, Robert. 1968. *Mound Builders of Ancient America, the Archaeology of a Myth*. Greenwich, Conn.: New York Graphic Society.

Smyth, Charles Piazzi. 1890. *Our Inheritance in the Great Pyramid*. London: Charles Burnet.

Sprague de Camp, L. 1974. *The Ancient Engineers*. New York: Ballantine Books.

Story, Ronald. 1977. *The Space–Gods Revealed*. New York: Barnes & Noble.

Stover, Leon E., and Bruce Kraig. 1978. *Stonehenge, the Indo–European Heritage*. Chicago: Nelson-Hall.

Struever, Stuart. 1964. "The Hopewell Interaction Sphere in Riverine–Western Great Lakes Culture History." In *Hopewellian Studies*, eds. J. R. Caldwell and R. L. Hall. Illinois State Museum Scientific Papers 12: 85–106.

Struever, Stuart, and Gail L. Houart, 1972. "An Analysis of the Hopewell Interaction Sphere." In *Social Exchange and Interaction*, ed. Edwin N. Wilmsen. Anthropological Papers, Museum of Anthropology, University of Michigan 46: 47–80.

Thom, A., and A. S. Thom. 1978. *Megalithic Remains in Britain and Brittany*. Oxford, England: Clarendon Press.

Tompkins, Peter. 1971. *Secrets of the Great Pyramid*. New York: Harper & Row.

Tompkins, Peter. 1976. *Mysteries of the Mexican Pyramids*. New York: Harper & Row.

Trigger, Bruce C. 1978. *Time and Traditions*. New York: Columbia University Press.

Urton, Gary. 1979. "Review of *Pathways to the Gods: The Mystery of the Andes Lines* by Tony Morrison." *Archaeoastronomy* 2 (4): 31–33.

Von Däniken, Erich. 1971. *Chariots of the Gods? Unsolved Mysteries of the Past*. New York: Bantam Books.

Von Däniken, Erich. 1972. *Gods from Outer Space*. New York: Bantam Books.

White, Peter. *The Past Is Human*. New York: Taplinger.

Willey, Gordon R. 1980. *The Social Uses of Archaeology*. The Kenneth B. Murdock Lecture. Cambridge, Mass.: Harvard University.

Willey, Gordon R., and Jeremy A. Sabloff. 1980. *A History of American Archaeology*. 2nd ed. San Francisco: W. H. Freeman and Company.

Wilson, Clifford. 1975. *The Chariots Still Crash*. New York: New American Library.

I

THE CHANGING NATURE OF ANTHROPOLOGICAL ARCHAEOLOGY

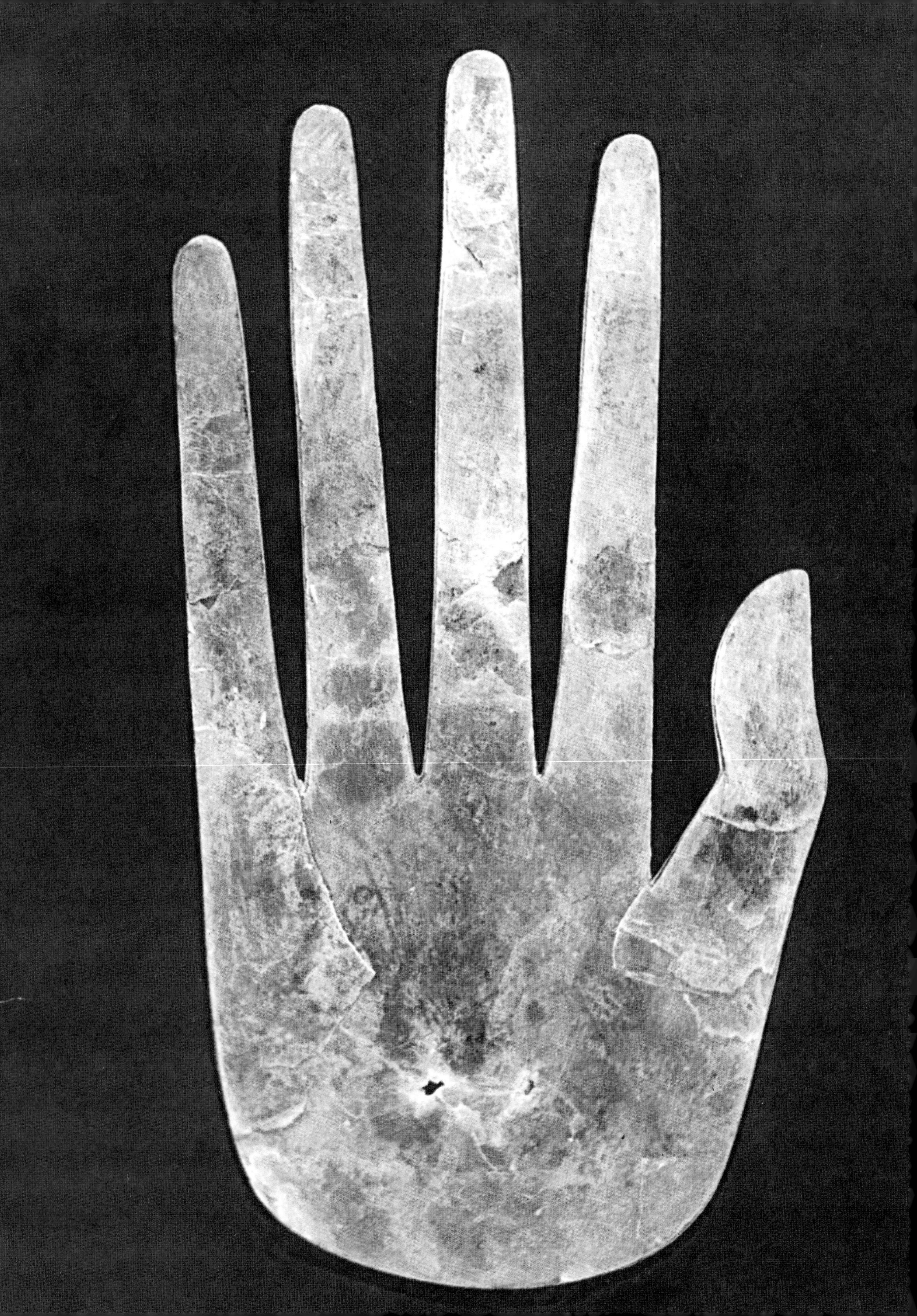

The Hopewell Cult

1

by Olaf H. Prufer
December 1964

A 1,500-year-old rubbish heap unearthed in southern Ohio holds the answers to some key questions about the ancient Indians who lived there and built huge funeral mounds filled with offerings

As Europeans explored North America, they found that many of the continent's river valleys were dotted with ancient earthworks. Scattered from western New York to North Dakota and south to Louisiana and the Florida Keys were uncounted thousands of burial mounds, temple mounds, hilltop ramparts surrounded by ditches, and earthen walls enclosing scores of acres. Some Colonial scholars were so impressed by these works that they thought they must have been built by an unknown civilized people that had been exterminated by the savage Indians. In due course it became clear that the earthworks had been put up by the Indians' own ancestors, and that they belonged not to one culture but to a series of separate cultural traditions spanning a period of 3,000 years.

Perhaps the most striking assemblage of these works is located in southern Ohio in the valleys of the Muskingum, Scioto and Miami rivers. It consists of clusters of large mounds surrounded by earthworks laid out in elaborate geometric patterns. As early as 1786 one such group of mounds at the confluence of the Muskingum and the Ohio (the present site of Marietta, Ohio) was excavated; it was found to be rich in graves and mortuary offerings. It was not until the 1890's, however, that the contents of the Ohio mounds attracted public attention. At that time many of them were excavated to provide an anthropological exhibit for the Chicago world's fair of 1893. One of the richest sites was on the farm of M. C. Hopewell, and the name Hopewell has been assigned to this particular type of mortuary complex ever since.

More recent excavations have shown that the Hopewell complex extends far beyond southern Ohio. Hopewell remains are found in Michigan and Wisconsin and throughout the Mississippi valley; there are Hopewell sites in Illinois that are probably older than any in Ohio. Typical Hopewell artifacts have been unearthed as far west as Minnesota and as far south as Florida. The mounds of southern Ohio are nonetheless the most numerous and the richest in mortuary offerings.

Thanks to carbon-14 dating it is known that the Hopewell complex first materialized in southern Ohio about 100 B.C. and that the last elaborate valley earthwork was constructed about A.D. 550. Until recently, however, there were other questions to which only conjectural answers could be given. Among them were the following: In what kinds of settlements did the people of southern Ohio live during this period? Where were their habitations located? On what foundation did their economy rest? Answers to these questions can now be given, but first it is necessary to say exactly what the Hopewell complex is.

What is known about the Hopewell complex of Ohio has been learned almost exclusively from the nature and contents of burial mounds. In many places these structures are found in groups enclosed by earthworks linked in a pattern of squares, circles, octagons and parallel lines [*see top illustration on page 30*]. The dimensions of some of the enclosures are immense: the largest known Hopewell earthworks in Ohio—the Newark Works in Licking County—covered four square miles. Many of the burial mounds are also large: the central mounds on the Hopewell farm and at the Seip and Harness sites, all of which are in Ross County, range from 160 to 470 feet in length and from 20 to 32 feet in height. Within the mounds are the remains of numerous human bodies, some of them alone and some in groups. If the bodies were simply interred, they rest on earthen platforms surrounded by log cribs; if they were cremated, the bones are found in shallow basins of baked earth.

The sequence of events in the construction of a major mound seems to have been as follows. Bare ground was first covered with a layer of sand; then a large wooden structure was raised on this prepared floor. Some of the structures were so extensive that it is doubtful that they had roofs; they were probably stockades open to the sky. Individual graves were prepared inside these enclosures; in many cases the burials were covered with low mounds of earth. When the enclosure was filled with graves, the wooden structure was set afire and burned to the ground. Then the entire burial area was covered with layer on layer of earth and stone, forming the final large mound.

The quantity and quality of the grave goods accompanying the burials indicate that the people of the period devoted a great deal of time and effort to making these articles. A marked preference for exotic raw materials is evident. Mica, frequently cut into geometric or animate shapes, was imported from the mountains of Virginia, North Carolina and Alabama [*see illustration on opposite page*]. Conch shells, used as ceremonial cups, came from the Gulf

SILHOUETTED HAND made from a sheet of mica (*opposite page*) is typical of the elaborate grave offerings found at the Hopewell site near Chillicothe, Ohio. Human, animal and geometric figures of mica are characteristic Hopewell funerary goods; they are particularly abundant in southern Ohio.

OCTAGON AND CIRCLE in this aerial photograph are a portion of the earthworks marking the most extensive known Hopewell construction: the site at Newark, Ohio. Most of the four-square-mile array (*see original plan below*) has now been obliterated by modern building. Only these figures (now part of a golf course) and another circle (used for years as a fairground) have been preserved.

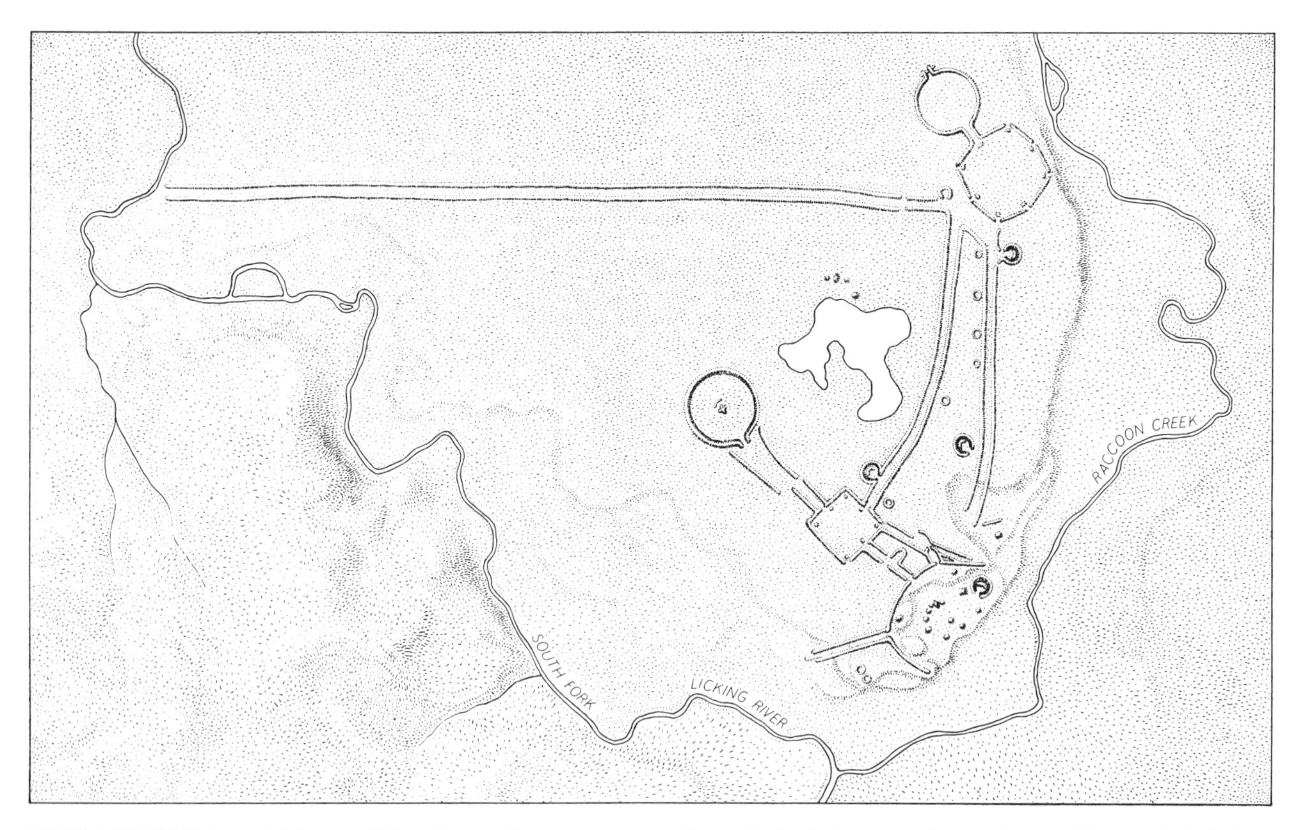

LONG AVENUES bounded by parallel earthen walls constitute the major parts of the Newark site. When first surveyed, the longest parallels (*top*) extended from the paired figures shown in the photograph at top of page to the Licking River, two and a half miles distant. Both circles are quite precise: the fairground circle (*center*) diverges at most 13 feet from a mean diameter of 1,175 feet, and the golf course circle only 4.5 feet from a mean diameter of 1,045 feet. The Newark site has never been systematically excavated.

Coast. Obsidian, exquisitely flaked into large ritual knives, was obtained either from what is now the U.S. Southwest or from the Yellowstone region of the Rocky Mountains. The canine teeth of grizzly bears, frequently inlaid with freshwater pearls, may also have been imported from the Rockies. Copper, artfully hammered into heavy ax blades and into ornaments such as ear spools, breastplates and geometric or animate silhouettes, was obtained from the upper Great Lakes.

Even in their choice of local raw materials the Hopewell craftsmen of Ohio favored the precious and the unusual. Much of their work in stone utilized the colorful varieties of flint available in the Flint Ridge deposits of Licking County. The freshwater pearls came from the shellfish of local rivers, and they were literally heaped into some of the burials. The tombs of the Hopewell site contained an estimated 100,000 pearls; a single deposit at the Turner site in Hamilton County has yielded more than 48,000.

Other typical Hopewell grave furnishings are "platform" pipes [*see lower illustration on page 34*], elaborately engraved bones of animals and men, clay figurines and highly distinctive kinds of decorated pottery. Projectile points of flint show characteristic forms; the flintworkers also struck delicate parallel-sided blades from prepared "cores."

For the most part these characteristic objects of the Hopewell complex are the same wherever they are found. In spite of this fact the Hopewell complex cannot be classed as a "culture" in the anthropological sense of the word, that is, as a distinct society together with its attendant material and spiritual manifestations. On the contrary, the Hopewell complex was only one segment of the cultural totality in each area where it is encountered. A reconstruction of life in eastern North America from 500 B.C. to A.D. 900 reveals the existence of distinct cultural traditions in separate regions, each rooted in its own past. During the Hopewell phase each of these regional traditions was independently influenced by the new and dynamic religious complex. The new funeral customs did not, however, take the place of the local culture; they were simply grafted onto it. Although the word "cult" has some unfortunate connotations in common usage, it is more appropriate to speak of a Hopewell cult than of a Hopewell culture.

The exact religious concepts that

EARTHWORKS characteristic of the burial cult are found throughout eastern North America. Major Hopewell centers, from the Gulf Coast to the Great Lakes, are named on the map.

SOUTHERN OHIO is the locale of the most abundant and richest Hopewell sites. The majority are found along the Miami, Scioto and Muskingum rivers and range in date from 100 B.C. to A.D. 550. After that no more lowland centers were built; instead hilltops were fortified (*colored dots locate three major examples*). The McGraw site was excavated by the author.

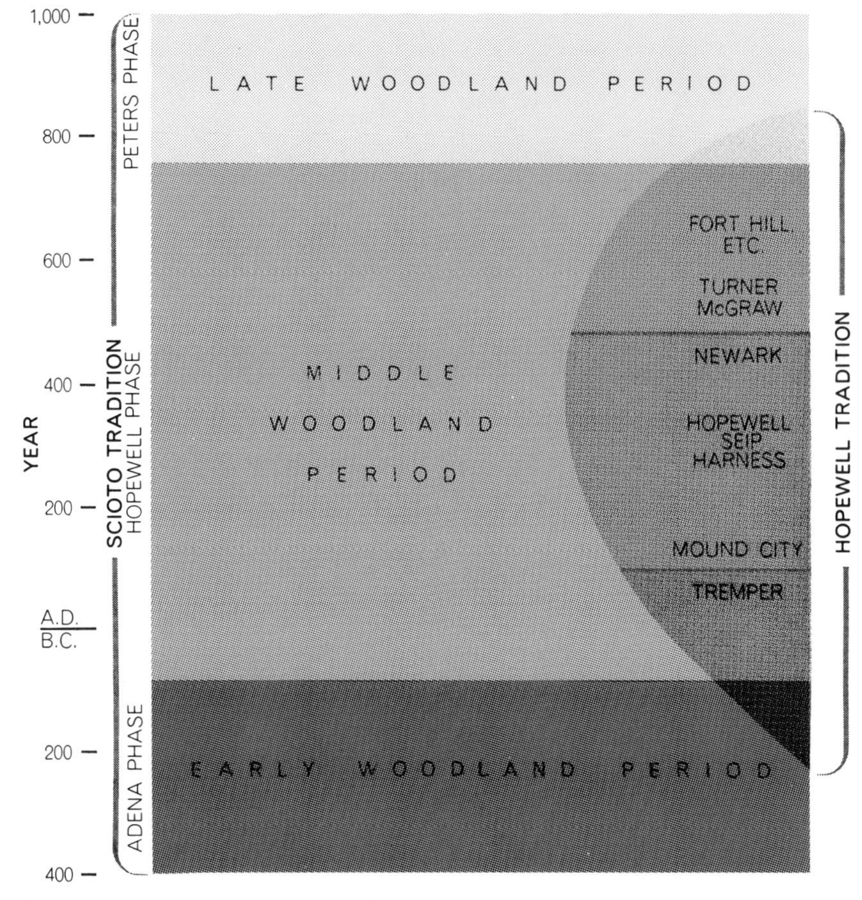

SEQUENCE OF CULTURES in southern Ohio during the rise and decline of the Hopewell funeral complex indicates that a local tradition of Woodland culture, called Scioto, was present in the area before the Hopewell cult appeared and continued both during and after it. The earliest of the Woodland culture periods began about 1200 B.C. in southern Ohio.

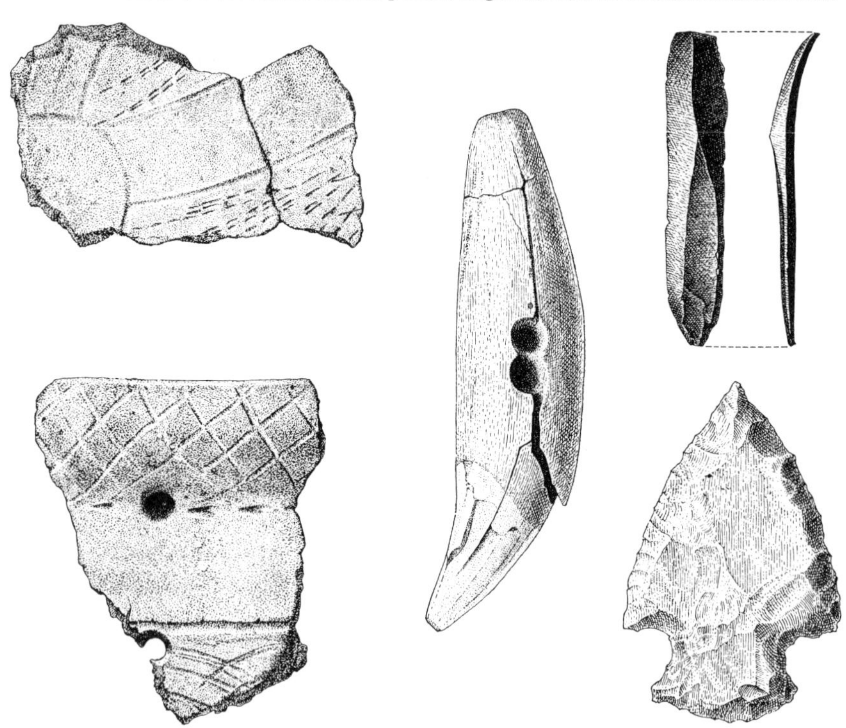

IDENTITY OF FARMSTEAD discovered at the McGraw site as the residence of Indians who participated in the burial cult is proved by the presence of characteristic Hopewell tools and ceremonial objects. The fine, parallel-sided flint blade is typically Hopewell, as is the "Snyders" projectile point. The bear canine and the pottery are standard burial finds.

permitted the successful diffusion of the Hopewell cult necessarily remain unknown. Curiously enough, however, the cult's consumption of exotic materials for grave goods may have provided a mechanism for its diffusion. Procurement of raw materials entailed an exchange system of almost continental proportions; many widely separated areas in North America must have been brought into contact as their natural resources were tapped by practitioners of the Hopewell rites.

Students of the Hopewell remains in southern Ohio have been disturbed for more than a century by the lack of evidence for any habitation sites linked to the great funerary centers. In other Hopewell areas, notably Illinois, large villages are clearly associated with the local ceremonial sites. Years of patient fieldwork in Ohio had failed to produce anything that could legitimately be called a settlement. The extensive enclosures and their associated clusters of burial mounds contain no evidence of habitation to speak of. The little that has been found seems to mark brief squatters' tenancies, probably associated with the construction of the final mounds or with ceremonies that may have been performed from time to time. Clearly the nature of Hopewell society and its settlement patterns in Ohio were markedly different from those in Illinois.

Still another puzzle was the fact that remains of corn have been found at only two Ohio Hopewell sites—Harness and Turner—and in both cases under doubtful circumstances. It was therefore supposed that the Hopewell phase in Ohio was one of simple hunting and collecting and no agriculture. Whether because of this supposition or because earlier investigators were looking for sizable villages, most of the search for Hopewell habitation sites has been confined to regions near the ceremonial centers, leaving the rich bottomlands along the rivers largely unexplored.

While reflecting on all these factors in 1962 I was struck by a possible parallel between the Ohio Hopewell sites and the classic ceremonial sites of certain areas in Middle America, where the religious center remained vacant except on ritual occasions and the population lived in scattered hamlets surrounding the center. To apply such an assumption to the Ohio Hopewell complex meant granting the people agriculture; it meant, furthermore, that the bottomlands were the very zones in which to look for small farming communities. Survey work along the floodplain of the middle and lower Scioto River during the past two years has amply demonstrated the validity of this assumption. Our survey teams from the Case Institute of Technology have turned up 37 small sites—the largest of them little more than 100 feet in diameter—marked by thinly scattered objects on the surface. These objects include sherds of cord-marked pottery, chips of flint, fragments of shell and bone and, most important, the fine, parallel-edged bladelets that are among the characteristic artifacts of the Hopewell complex.

It is certain that many such habitation sites are now lost forever under the accumulated silt of river floodplains and that others have been destroyed by river meandering. A perfect example of flood burial in the making is provided by the McGraw site, which is located on bottomland near an ancient meander of the Scioto River two miles south of Chillicothe. Alva McGraw, the owner of the land, brought the site to our attention in 1962. Surface indications were scanty; over an area 10 feet square we found only a few potsherds, some shell fragments, bits of flint and fire-cracked rocks. The site was on a nearly imperceptible rise of land, the remnant of a knoll that had been almost covered by river silts.

Under ordinary circumstances no archaeologist would have been attracted by such an impoverished find. It happened, however, that this site and similar ones on the McGraw farm were soon to be destroyed by road construction. We therefore decided without much enthusiasm to sound the area with a modest trench. Where the trench cut into the ancient knoll we found no remains at depths lower than the plow zone: eight inches below the surface. But where the trench extended beyond the knoll, proceeding down its slope to the adjacent silt-covered low ground, we struck a dense deposit of residential debris, evidently the refuse heap of an ancient farmstead.

This deposit, a foot thick and 95 by 140 feet in extent, was packed with material. There were more than 10,000 pottery fragments, some 6,000 animal bones, nearly 2,000 identifiable mollusk shells, abundant remains of wild plants and both an ear and individual kernels of corn. In fact, this single rubbish heap contained enough material to answer the questions posed at the beginning of this article.

First, in spite of the pattern of organized village life associated with the Hopewell cult 400 miles to the west in Illinois, the people of southern Ohio lived in small, scattered farm dwellings. This does not mean that the population was sparse; indeed, the size and complexity of the ceremonial earthworks in Ohio imply ample manpower. The significant fact is that the two groups shared a religion but lived quite different secular lives. In seeking parallels for this phenomenon one turns to the early, expansionist days of Christianity or of Islam, when a religion was shared by peoples with sharply contrasting cultures.

Second, the Ohio Hopewell people built their dwellings not near ceremonial centers but on the floodplains of the

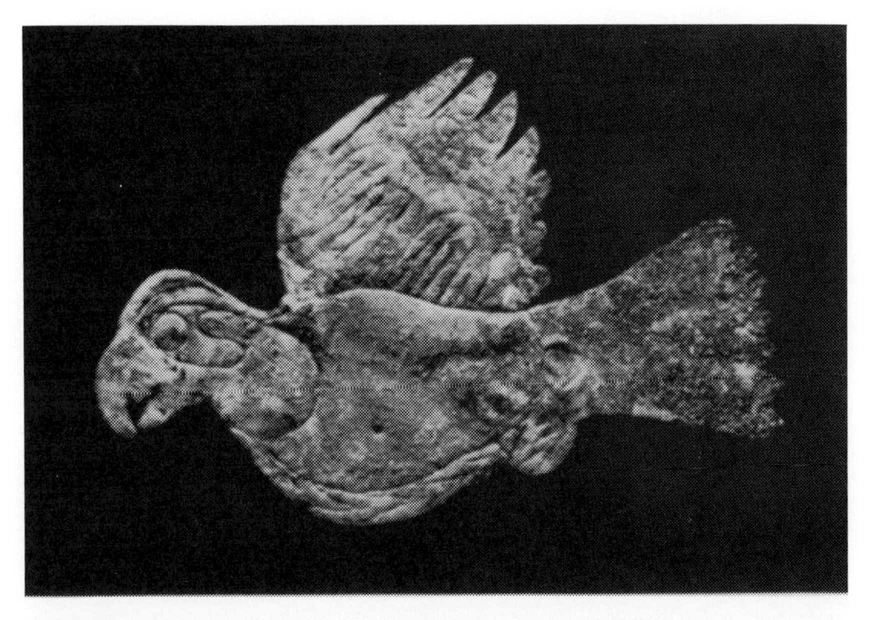

BIRD EFFIGY from Mound City combines cutout and repoussé techniques in copper work. The metal was imported from outcroppings at Isle Royale in Lake Superior. Hopewell funeral offerings of copper include rings, ear spools, breastplates and headdresses, many geometric forms, copper-plated wooden objects and large ax blades, evidently cold-forged.

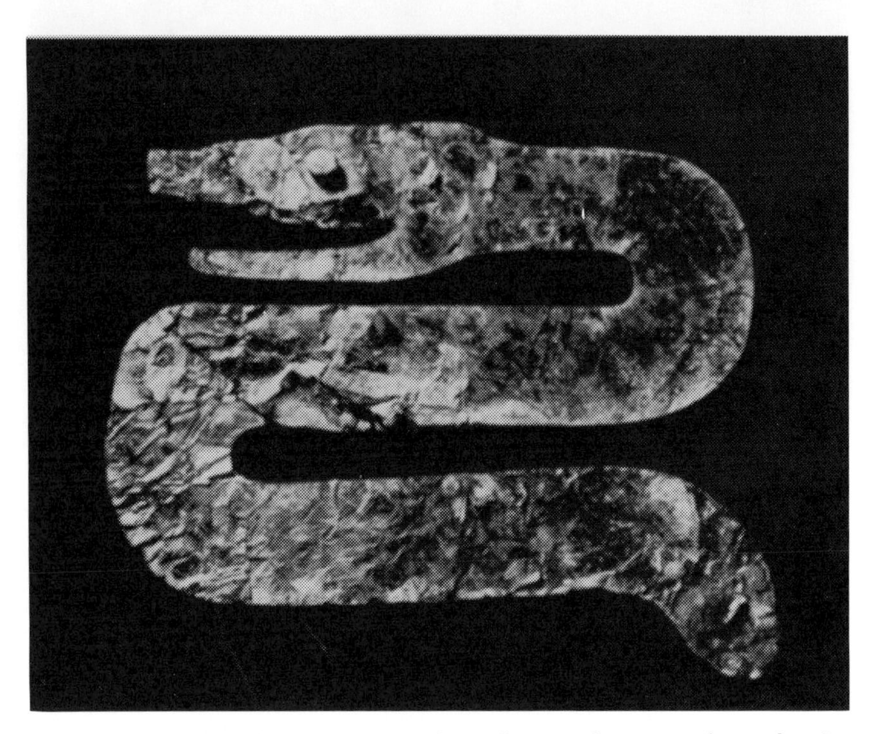

SNAKE EFFIGY from the Turner site is a foot-wide mica silhouette cut from a sheet imported from Virginia or North Carolina. Some Ohio burials were literally blanketed by mica.

HUMAN FIGURES representing a kneeling man and a standing woman are modeled in terra-cotta. Unearthed at the Turner site, they were ritually broken, or "killed," before burial.

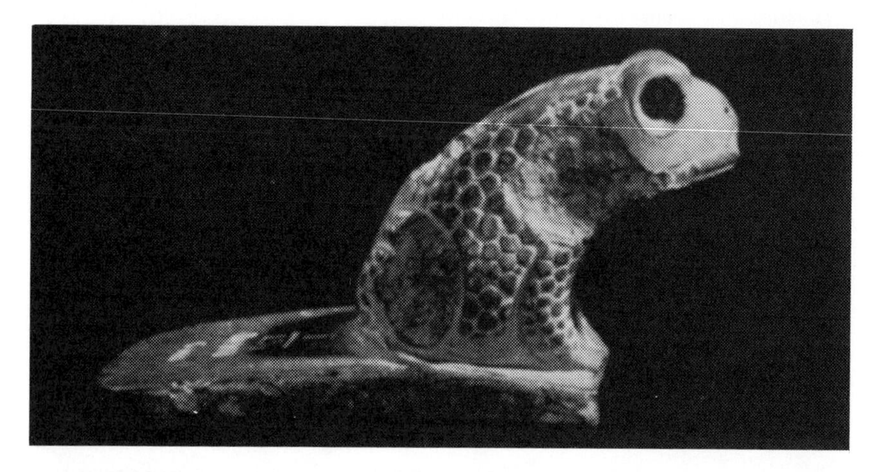

PLATFORM PIPE from the Mound City site has a bowl carved to represent a toad. Pipes showing birds, fishes, mammals and human figures were also made for Hopewell burials.

rivers, presumably because the bottomland was most suitable for agriculture. As for their economy in general, they raised corn, but a substantial part of their food came from hunting, fishing and collecting. Analysis of the animal bones in the McGraw deposit shows that the commonest source of meat was the white-tailed deer. Other game animals that have been identified in the deposit are the cottontail rabbit and the turkey. River produce was of equal or perhaps greater importance for the larder; we found the bones and shells of a variety of turtles, the bones of nine species of fish and the shells of 25 species of mollusk.

Among the wild-plant foods these people collected were nuts: the deposit contained charred remains of hickory nuts, walnuts and acorns. Other wild plants that have been identified are the hackberry and the wild plum. Apparently corn was the only plant the people cultivated, but the remains make it clear that their knowledge of corn-raising had not been recently acquired. The charred ear of corn from the McGraw site, still bearing a number of kernels, is of a 12-row variety. It appears to be of a type intermediate between the northern flint corn grown in Ohio in late pre-European times and the ancient flint corns and popcorns known from elsewhere in the Western Hemisphere. One of the isolated kernels from the deposit has been identified as belonging to an eight-row or 10-row variety of corn; it possibly represents a full-fledged, although small, member of the northern flint type. These relatively advanced types of corn imply a long period of agricultural activity before the site was first occupied.

The date of the McGraw site's occupation can be estimated both from the style of its artifacts and from carbon-14 determinations; it is roughly A.D. 450. The bulk of the artifacts could have come from any pre-Hopewell site in Ohio; for example, less than 4 percent of the pottery fragments found in the deposit are characteristic of the Hopewell complex. This reinforces the point made earlier: Whenever the influences of the Hopewell cult appear, they are imposed on an already existing culture that for the most part continues in its own ways.

The McGraw site is nevertheless clearly identified as belonging to the Hopewell complex not only by the few Hopewell potsherds but also by other characteristic Hopewell artifacts. Parallel-sided flint bladelets were found in large numbers, and the bulk of the projectile points were of the classic Hopewell type known as "Snyders," after the site of that name in Illinois. The inhabitants of the McGraw farmstead evidently included craftsmen engaged in the production of grave goods for the Hopewell cult: cut and uncut mica was found in abundance. One bear tooth turned up in the midden, with typical countersunk perforations but without any inlay of pearls. There were also two ornaments made of slate that, like the bear-tooth ornament, were unfinished. Perhaps all these objects were discards; this would help to explain their presence in a refuse heap.

The McGraw site therefore casts considerable light on life in southern Ohio

CEREMONIAL BLADES unearthed at the Hopewell site are of obsidian, probably from the Yellowstone area of the Rocky Mountains. The largest (*center*) is 13 inches in length.

during the latter days of the Hopewell phase. Skilled hunters and food-collectors, gifted artisans in a wide range of materials, the people who manufactured the rich grave goods for the ritual burials lived in small scattered farmsteads on the river bottoms.

But were the people who made the grave goods the same as those who were buried in the great Hopewell mounds? Curiously this appears to be unlikely, at least in southern Ohio. To explain why, it is necessary to sketch what is known about the rise and decline of the Hopewell complex against the general background of the various prehistoric cultures in eastern North America.

Of the four successive major culture stages in this part of the New World—Paleo-Indian, Archaic, Woodland and Mississippian—only the third is involved here. In southern Ohio the Woodland stage begins about 1200 B.C. and ends shortly before the arrival of the Europeans. In the entire eastern part of North America, southern Ohio included, the Woodland stage is divided into Early, Middle and Late periods.

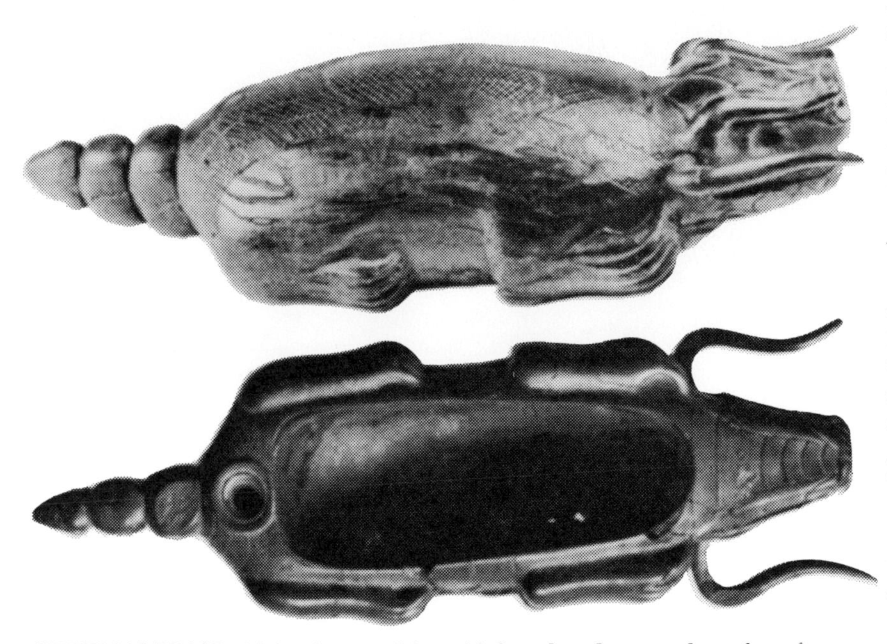

MYTHICAL BEAST with four horns and feet with five talons decorates the surface of a narrow stone object 10 inches long. It was found at the Turner site. Its purpose is unknown.

In southern Ohio the people of the Early Woodland period were mound builders long before the Hopewell cult arose. They belonged to the Adena culture (which takes its name from a mound site near Chillicothe). The remains of the Adena people show that they were roundheaded rather than longheaded. They lived without contact with the Hopewell cult until about 100 B.C.; at that time, according to carbon-14 determinations, the Tremper mound of Scioto County was raised. This mound contained some 300 crematory burials. Many of the grave offerings are typical of the Adena culture, but some of them show Hopewell influences.

As skulls from later burials indicate, the arrival of the Hopewell cult in Ohio (presumably from Illinois) was accompanied by the arrival of a new population; these people were longheaded rather than roundheaded. How many immigrants arrived is an open question. The total number of individuals found in Ohio Hopewell mounds—an estimated 1,000—can represent only a fraction of the population of this region during the Middle Woodland period. It seems probable that most of the local inhabitants were the roundheaded Adena folk, many of whom may well have continued to live typical Adena lives untroubled by the neighboring Hopewell cultists. The fact that numerous Adena mounds continued to be built during Hopewell times is strong evidence for this.

To judge from their production of Hopewell ceremonial objects, the residents of the McGraw site would not have been undisturbed Adena folk. It is equally unlikely that they were immigrants from Illinois. It seems more probable that the immigrants were a privileged minority who in some way had come to dominate some of Ohio's Adena people, among whom were the farmers of the McGraw site.

Why did the Hopewell complex ultimately disappear? It may be that one part of the answer is plain to see. From their first arrival in southern Ohio until A.D. 550 these cultists evidently not only felt secure in themselves but also appear to have taken no steps to guard from raiders the treasures buried with their dead. After that time, however, no more ceremonial centers were built in open valleys. Instead it seems that every inaccessible hilltop in southern Ohio was suddenly crowned by earthworks that appear to have served a defensive function.

This does not mean that such sites as

Fort Hill, Fort Ancient and Fort Miami were permanently inhabited strongholds. Quite the contrary; at Fort Hill, for example, a survey of the land surrounding the foot of the hill has revealed several small farmsteads resembling the McGraw site. It is probable that the hilltop earthworks were places of refuge that were occupied only in time of danger. That there were such times is demonstrated by the evidence of fires and massacres at the Fort Hill, Fort Ancient and Fort Miami sites.

What was the nature of the danger? As yet there is no answer, but it is interesting to note that at about this same time the Indian population in more northerly areas first began to protect their villages with stockades. Unrest of some kind appears to have been afoot throughout eastern North America.

This being the case, it is not hard to envision the doom of the Hopewell cult. Whatever its basic religious tenets, the tangible elements of the ceremony were the celebrated grave goods, and the most notable of the goods were produced from imported raw materials. The grave goods were of course cherished for their part in the religious scheme; could the scheme itself be kept alive when the goods were no longer available? I suggest that the Hopewell cult could survive only as long as its trade network remained intact and, further, that the postulated current of unrest in eastern North America during the seventh and eighth centuries A.D. was sufficient to disrupt that network.

Whether or not this caused the collapse of the Hopewell cult, there is no question that it did collapse. By the beginning of the Late Woodland period, about A.D. 750, elaborate burial mounds containing rich funeral offerings were no longer built. For the very reason that Hopewell was only a cult and not an entire culture, however, the distinctive local traditions that had participated in the Hopewell ceremonies now reasserted themselves.

In Ohio this regional tradition is named Scioto [*see top illustration on page 32*]. Because of the alien nature of the Hopewell ceremonial complex, the phase of the Scioto tradition—called Hopewell—during which the funeral centers were built has a dual status. In terms of chronology the Hopewell phase was only one subdivision of the Scioto tradition. At the same time the Hopewell religious cult must be granted the status of a full-fledged tradition in its own right.

II

STONEHENGE

Stonehenge

2

by Jacquetta Hawkes
June 1953

The strange monument is often attributed to the Druids of 2,000 years ago, but radiocarbon dating supports the view that it was started by a savage but aspiring people 2,000 years before that

THE GREAT prehistoric sanctuary of Stonehenge stands among the sweeping curves of the chalk downland of Salisbury Plain. Not very many miles away on a more northern stretch of the Wiltshire downs is Avebury—another most remarkable though less famous stone circle. Around both Avebury and Stonehenge cluster vast numbers of burial mounds, many of them the graves of wealthy Bronze Age chieftains whose presence there is proof of the fame and sanctity of these circles in ancient times.

The architecture of Stonehenge is arresting in its strangeness. Nowhere in the world is there anything quite comparable to this temple, built not of masonry but of colossal rectangular blocks of stone. Plainly it is the handiwork of a people more barbaric than any of historic times, yet the careful shaping of the huge monoliths, the use of horizontal lintel stones, and above all the coherence of the whole as a work of architecture set it far above the usual megalithic building of prehistoric western Europe.

It is no wonder, then, that for the past thousand years Stonehenge has been so famous as to attract countless visitors and speculation of every kind. Among the many famous men who went there were Inigo Jones, Samuel Pepys, John Evelyn and William Wordsworth—indeed Wordsworth has enriched its literature with poetry of the first rank. James I knew it and was curious about its origin; Charles II, when he was sheltering at nearby Amesbury after the battle of Worcester, spent a day there counting and measuring the stones to pass the time and forget his anxieties.

Today more than ever Stonehenge attracts its visitors. Summer tourists go there in thousands, leaving buses and cars to buy tickets at a Ministry of Works kiosk and approaching this holy place of their forebears along a path flanked by neat waste-paper baskets. Even in these conditions, once inside the circle visitors surrender to the power of its stones. In spite of our familiarity with architecture on a vastly greater scale, there is something about these massive, weather-beaten monoliths which awes modern men with thoughts of a savage, primitive, yet mightily aspiring world.

We know that immediately after the Norman Conquest Stonehenge was rec-

HEEL STONE is seen from within the circles of Stonehenge. Sir Norman Lockyer tried to date the monument by computing that on Midsummer Day (June 24) in 1680 B.C. the sun rose directly over the Heel Stone.

ognized as one of the wonders of Britain. The fanciful 12th-century historian Geoffrey of Monmouth suggested that the stones had been fetched to Salisbury Plain from Ireland by the wizard Merlin in the days of Ambrosius, the uncle of King Arthur. Subsequently, he said, the circles were used as the burial place of Ambrosius and his brother, Uther Pendragon, Arthur's father.

This tale was believed all through medieval times and was repeated with variations by writers in Latin, French and English. By the 16th-century Renaissance scholarship was harshly and sometimes mockingly questioning Geoffrey of Monmouth and the whole glorious but improbable Arthurian legend. But the new scholars and antiquaries hardly knew whom to put in Merlin's place as the founder of Stonehenge. During the 16th, 17th and 18th centuries this baffling inheritance from the past was attributed to the Romans, Danes, Phoenicians and Druids. Most of these theorists recognized it as a temple, but one school of thought (the Danish) identified it as a crowning place of kings.

TODAY we are inclined to smile at all these notions; we can supply dates and attach archaeological labels that look convincing enough. The truth is, however, that we still have not explained the unique architecture of Stonehenge. Stone circles are a special feature of prehistoric Britain. They are found all the way from the south of England to the extreme north of Scotland, where there are fine examples in the Orkneys. Some of them are circles of free-standing stones; others are enclosed by a circular bank and ditch. These circles are all assumed to be holy places, and all can be said to have some relationship with Stonehenge. But how inferior they are! Even Avebury cannot compare with the architectural grandeur of Stonehenge.

It is not surprising that Avebury and Stonehenge, the two most imposing circles in Britain, should both be situated on the Wiltshire downs. As geographers have often pointed out, this region forms the hub of the uplands system of southern England, and it was on these uplands that prehistoric settlement was most strongly concentrated. Throughout almost the whole of prehistoric times the English lowlands were made largely uninhabitable and impassable by the heavy growth of oak forest. The early farmers sought the chalk and limestone hills, where the thin, light soil could readily be cleared to improve pasturage and make room for their small grain plots.

On the broad chalk plateau of Salisbury Plain and the adjacent Marlborough Downs many lines of hills converge—the Cotswolds and their northern prolongation up to Yorkshire, the Chilterns, North and South Downs, Dorset Downs and Mendips. The plateau therefore early achieved the dominance usual to centers of communication. Not only were the pastoral tribesmen of this area sufficiently prosperous to be able to afford the prodigious expenditure of labor needed to build Stonehenge and Avebury, but they were able to build them in places accessible to the whole of England south of the Pennines. They may have been able to draw labor or tribute from such a wide area, but whether or not this was the case we can be reasonably confident that the sanctuaries served as rallying points. At the most important seasonal festivals tribesmen must surely have traveled to them along the ridgeways of all the radiating hills. There is interesting evidence for such a gathering of peoples in the occurrence of grave goods of a kind characteristic of the north of England in at least one of the barrow burials lying close to Stonehenge.

LIKE MANY Gothic cathedrals, Stonehenge is a composite structure in which feature was added to feature through the centuries. This structure includes several important parts in addition to the circles of standing stones which are what most people mean when they speak of Stonehenge. Before going on to discuss the history of the monument it will be well first to describe its parts [*see diagram on page 44*].

To the north of the sanctuary, stretches the great length of the Cursus, a very narrow embanked enclosure some 1¾ miles long. It owes its odd name to the 18th-century antiquary William Stukeley, who liked to fancy that it served as a course for chariot racing. It is easy to laugh at Stukeley's fantasy, but the actual purpose of this and the few other enclosures of the kind in southern England remains unexplained. What is of particular interest for an understanding of Stonehenge itself lies in a recent discovery made at the west end of the Cursus, at the point where the side banks appear to terminate against a long burial mound. In this area excavation and field survey discovered a strong concentration of chippings from the Blue Stones which now form a part of the sanctuary itself. It has therefore been suggested that these stones, known from other evidence to have been present in the area before they were erected in their present sockets, originally stood here at the west end of the Cursus.

The other important outlying earthwork associated with Stonehenge is the Avenue, which can be assumed to have been the main ceremonial approach to the sanctuary. It consists of two parallel lines of bank and ditch about 70 feet apart which, from the northeast side of the circles, run almost dead straight for 1,800 feet, then swing eastward and curve gradually toward the River Avon. The banks and ditches are now so nearly level as to be clearly visible only from the air.

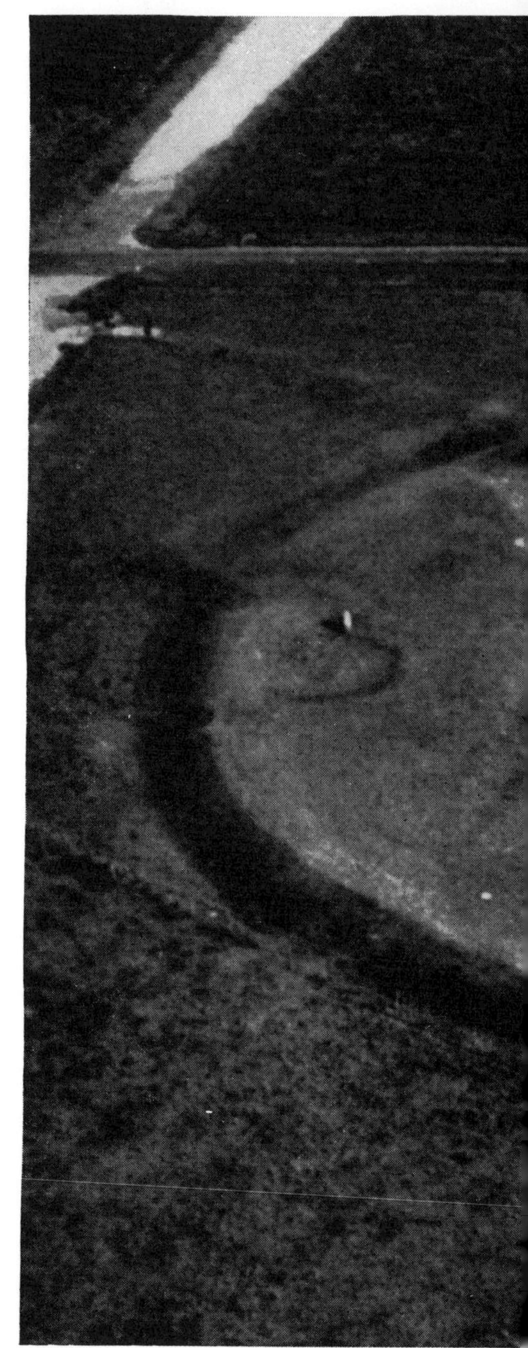

AERIAL VIEW of the monument shows how its stones are encircled

A circular embankment about 320 feet in diameter encloses the sanctuary itself. Such an enclosing bank and ditch is the feature which is held to distinguish a "henge" from an ordinary free-standing stone circle. Immediately inside the bank is a ring of pits, named the Aubrey Holes after their 17-century discoverer. They are 56 in number and all roughly circular. Cremation burials, without urns and normally without grave goods, were found in many Aubrey Holes and also in a quadrant of the ditch and bank.

Between the Aubrey Holes and the

by a bank and a ditch. The small white circles within the bank mark those Aubrey Holes which have been excavated. At the upper right is the Avenue, which runs straight for 1,800 feet and then curves toward the Avon.

stone circles are two more rings of pits, long known to archaeology as the Y and Z Holes; the individual pits are oval and about six feet long.

AFTER THIS account of the earthworks and ceremonial pits associated with the monument, we can leave these painfully unspectacular but historically important features and approach the stones themselves. Those that first catch the attention are the immense sarsens, great monoliths of sandstone. The nearest place from which blocks of this size could have been obtained apparently is the Avebury region, miles away, and the transport of the some 80 sarsens at Stonehenge, running up to 30 feet in length and weighing an average of 28 tons each, was a prodigious effort, especially as the journey necessitated the crossing of a broad, soft-bottomed and overgrown valley. Presumably they were dragged on rollers by men hauling on rawhide ropes.

The sarsen architecture of Stonehenge has two parts: an outer circle about 100 feet in diameter and an inner horseshoe formed of five gateways. The circle originally had 30 columns, united by a continuous lintel of smaller blocks laid over their tops. The stones are all roughly squared, and the lintel stones are secured onto the uprights by tenons and sockets, and to one another by mortise joints. The chopping out of two tenons on the top of each upright and of the rails of the mortise joints is a remarkable achievement for masons working only with clumsy stone mauls. The largest sarsens of all are found in the inner horseshoe, which measures 44 feet across and 50 feet along the axial line. Its colossal central gateway is more than 25 feet high.

THE SARSEN peristyle and horseshoe setting astound us by their size and the unparalleled precision of their masonry; they please the eye, too, by their soft gray color and the richness of texture produced by the weathering of the sandstone. Yet it is the other element of this extraordinary monument that can claim the most fascinating and dramatic history. The plan of the outer circle and horseshoe of sarsens is repeated on a smaller scale by a circle and horseshoe of the so-called Blue Stones. These stones are very much smaller and they lack the architectural refinement of lintels. What is so astonishing about them is that they were made from rocks (mainly dolerites and rhyolites) which are found together only in the Presely Mountains in the extreme west of Wales. It is equally astonishing whether one thinks of the immense physical difficulties of their transport from Wales to southern England or of the sanctity which must have resided in them to prompt prehistoric men to undertake such a feat.

The question of the route by which the stones were carried has been much disputed. Perhaps the most satisfactory view is that they came by sea (probably from Milford Haven in the west of Wales) to the mouth of the Bristol Avon and were then conveyed across Somerset and Wiltshire by a series of rivers close enough together to require only short portages. This seems the easiest route—but even so the distance involved is well over 300 miles. Across the innermost tip of the Blue Stone horseshoe lies a single so-called Altar Stone. This supposed Altar Stone, which in fact may formerly have stood upright, is made of a variety of sandstone found near Milford Haven.

THE layout of the complicated sanctuary at once suggests different periods of construction for its parts. The enclosing embankment and the Aubrey

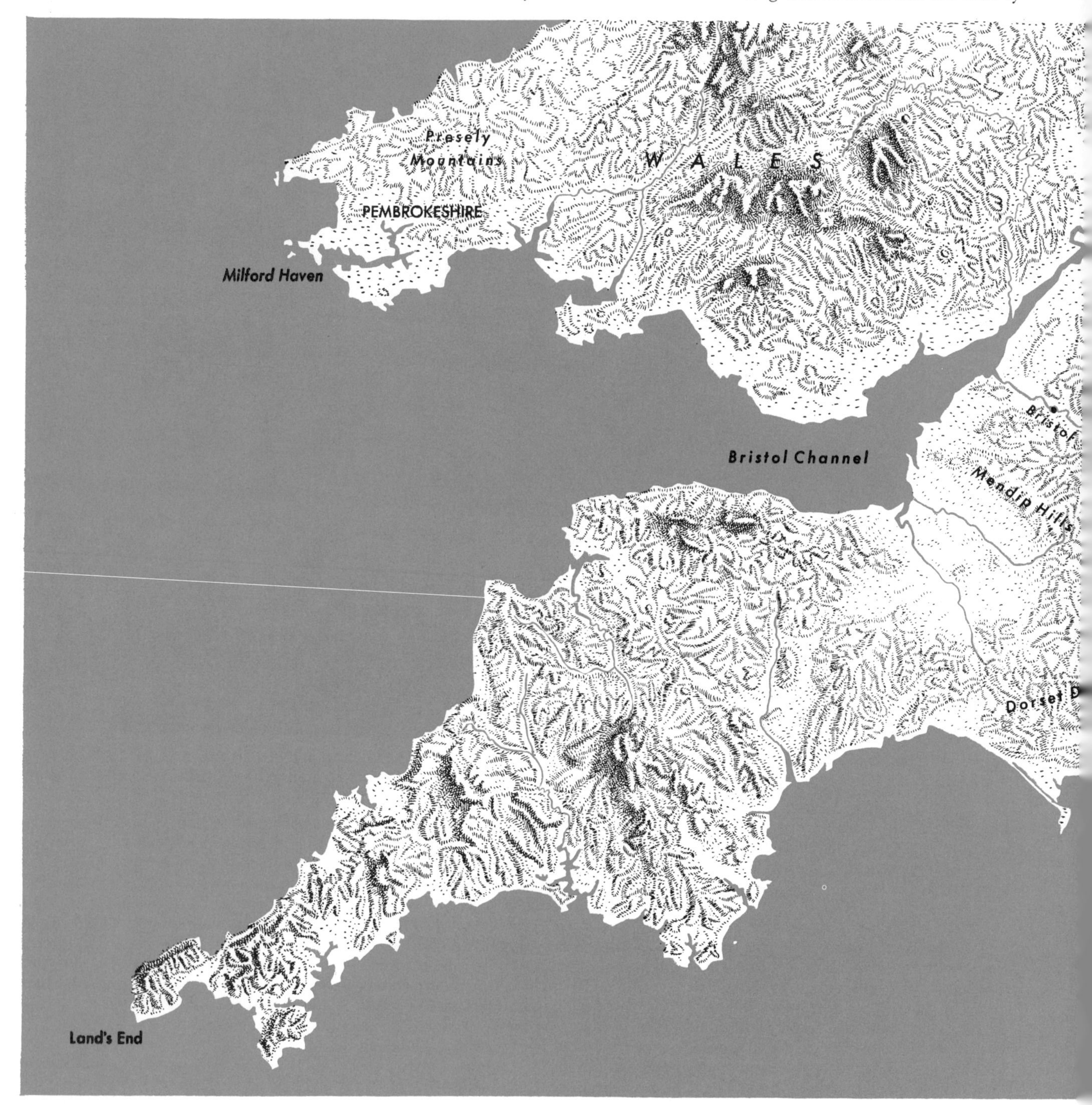

RELIEF MAP of southern England and Wales shows the geography which influenced the location of Stonehenge. When the monument was built, the English lowlands were covered with a thick oak forest; the early

Holes have one common center, while the stone structure is very precisely centered on a different point, a foot or two from the center of the earthwork. The axis of the stone complex as marked by the horseshoes falls exactly along the center line of the Avenue but considerably to one side of the entrance causeway through the earthwork. As for the Y and Z Holes, they are set in irregular arcs as though the distances had been measured not from a true center but by estimation from the outer sarsen circle.

Thus the plan suggests that the enclosure and Aubrey Holes are of one age, the stone structure and the Avenue of a second, and the Y and Z Holes of a third. Excavation and analysis of many kinds have proved this division to be correct, and furthermore that this order in fact represents their correct chronological sequence. They have also shown that the Cursus belongs to the earliest period, being approximately contemporary with the enclosure and Aubrey Holes.

ALTHOUGH many difficulties and uncertainties still remain, years of digging and research have at last made it possible to give a coherent account of the long history of Stonehenge. The first building period is now generally recognized as belonging to a late neolithic culture. These tribesmen dug the long entrenchments of the Cursus, the enclosure ditch with its single entrance and the ritual pits within. Just before or after the making of these very humble earthworks they transported the Blue Stones and Altar Stone from Wales. As these stones must already have been imbued with a most compelling religious value, it can be assumed that they had formed part of a sacred monument in Wales. They were set up at some spot

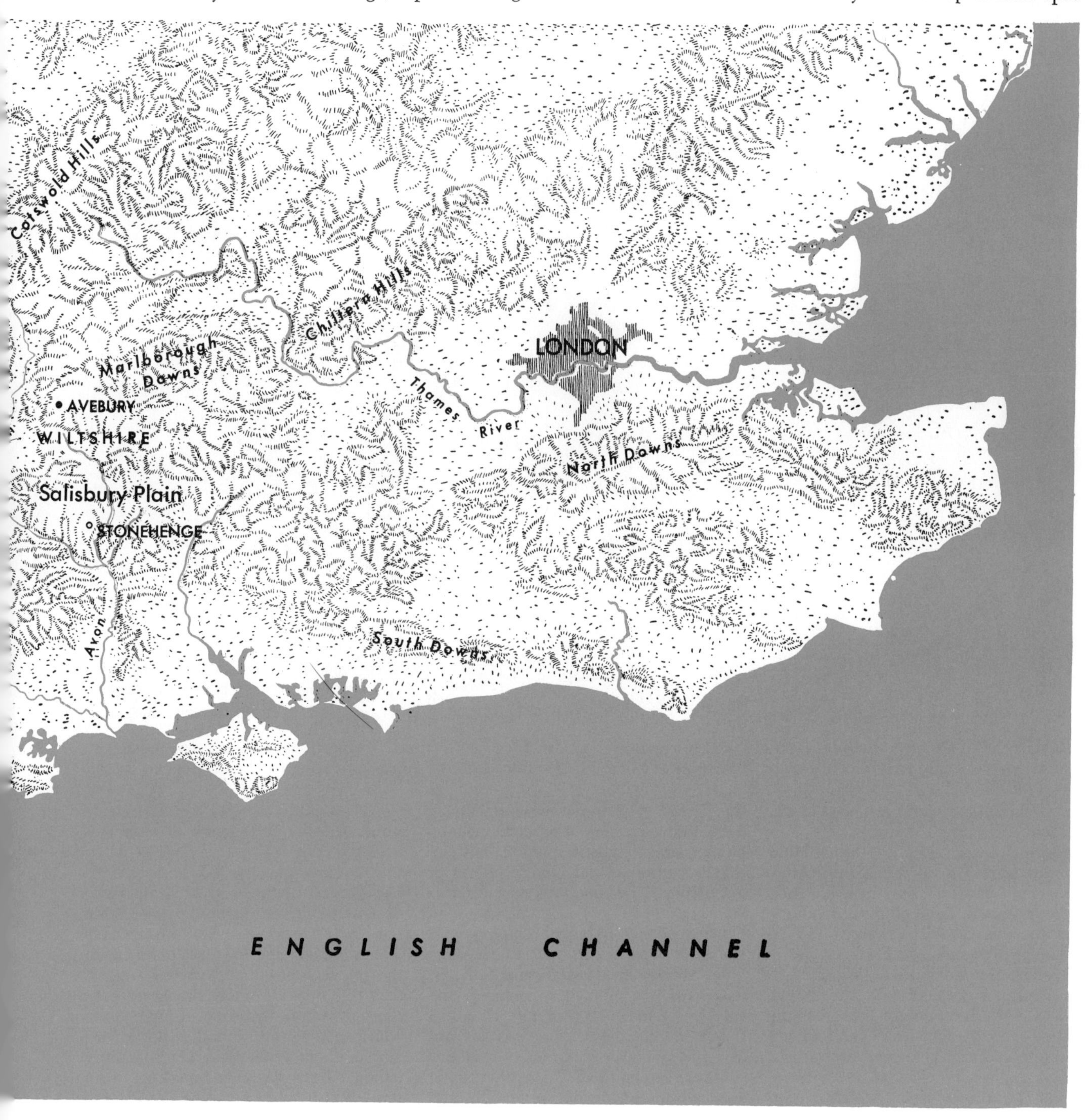

farmers thus sought the thinly covered chalk and limestone hills of Wiltshire. Some of the stones for the monument came from the Presely Mountains in Wales by way of the Bristol Channel or around Land's End.

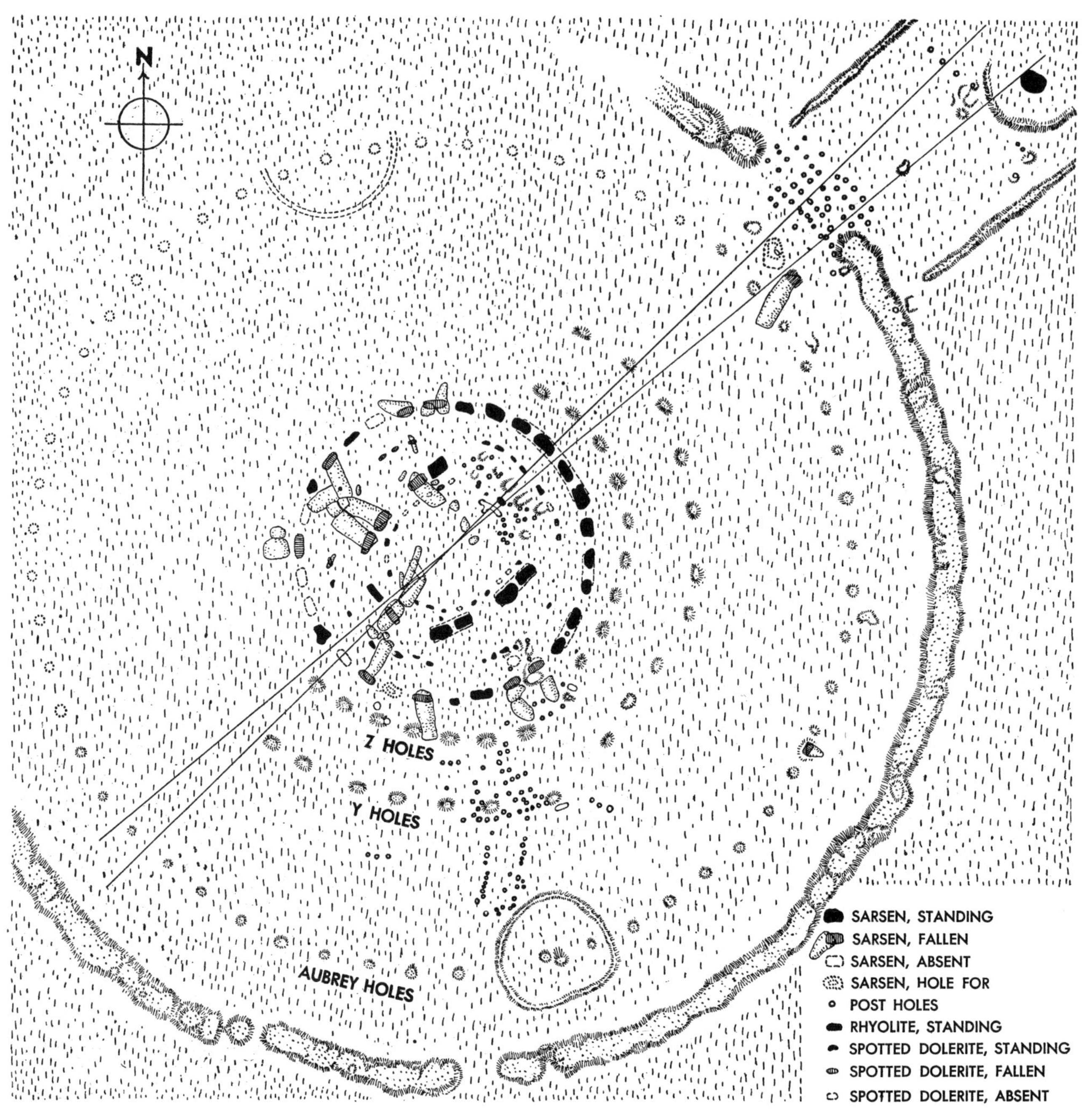

GROUND PLAN of Stonehenge shows its stones both in their present and original positions. The axes of both the large and small horseshoes are aligned with the Avenue, but the main entrance to the enclosure is not.

which may or may not have been at the western end of the Cursus.

During this earliest phase the neolithic peoples were already using the monument for cremation burials—a practice which seems to have continued unbroken into the second phase.

This first Stonehenge has been dated by British archaeologists as belonging to the centuries immediately after 2000 B.C. It was exceedingly gratifying to them to have their historical findings confirmed recently by radiocarbon dating of a piece of charcoal taken from one of the Aubrey Holes, which gave a date of about 1845 B.C., with a possible margin of error of 275 years.

The second period of Stonehenge, the period of its greatness, appears to have followed upon the first with no greater break than is implied between the Romanesque and Gothic phases of a cathedral. The enormous sarsen blocks were dragged from the Marlborough Downs, given their final shaping with stone mauls and set in position; the Blue Stone monument was dismantled and its pieces reassembled to enhance the sanctity of the new building. At much the same time the Avenue was laid out as a ceremonial way. Cremation burials continued to be made inside the sacred area, while outside it the wealthy and powerful men and women of the tribe were buried with their gold, their scepters of office and other precious possessions below the barrows which still ride so majestically upon many of the neighboring downs.

For the exact period and cultural background of the men of genius who designed this second Stonehenge there is no direct evidence. Certain elements which Stonehenge has in common with the relevant phase at Avebury suggest that this, like the more northern sanctuary, was built by beaker-using peoples who began to invade and settle in Britain in about 1800 B.C. On the other hand, it has been very tempting to assume that the building was done by the people of the Bronze Age Wessex culture, whose leaders lie buried in the richest of the associated barrow graves, and in whose time (about 1450 B.C.) the power and prosperity of the Salisbury Plain region was at its height.

AS FOR the uses for which this great building was raised, there is no possibility of doubting that it was a sacred place, and little need, except for the excessively cautious or scholastic, to refrain from calling it a temple. There is no question, either, that its orientation was dictated by the position of the midsummer sunrise. The axis of the second Stonehenge points to the spot where the sun would have risen at the summer solstice during the first half of the second millennium before Christ.

If in its second phase the monument reached its glory, in its third phase it must have presented a melancholy picture of decay. It would hardly be possible to claim anything better for a period represented by the Y and Z Holes, and possibly by a single inhumed burial! It is not known for what purpose these Y and Z Holes were dug, for they appear never to have held either posts or standing stones.

That they were dug after the stone circle was already tumbling into decay is clearly shown by at least one piece of evidence. One of the big sarsens of the outer stone circle has fallen across the Z circle, and there is no hole beneath the stone, although the spacing of the Z Holes indicates that one should have been there. It seems plain enough that it could not be dug because the stone already blocked the way.

Pieces of pottery found in the pits suggest that the Y and Z Holes date from the Celtic Iron Age, probably from about the second century B.C. If this is so, it is more than likely that they represent a very limited attempt to restore the use of the sanctuary after a long period of decay covering all the latter part of the Bronze Age. This Iron Age revival makes it permissible to say that perhaps by good luck Stukeley may not have been altogether wrong when he spread the idea, still too widely held, that Stonehenge was the handiwork of the Celtic priesthood of the Druids. Build it they most certainly did not, but they may conceivably have officiated there before the ancient sanctuary was abandoned and left to turn into a noble ruin.

AS WE have seen, the history of Stonehenge did not end with its abandonment. If we take a unified view of history, Stonehenge is no less important as a subject for countless chroniclers and many poets, as a place visited by Pepys and where Charles II whiled away an afternoon after the battle of Worcester, than it is as the greatest sanctuary of prehistoric Europe. Certainly we can say that if in the Bronze Age it was known throughout Britain, today it is famous all around the world.

VARIOUS ASPECTS of Stonehenge are shown by these photographs. The monument is seen from the east (*top*), southeast (*middle*) and northwest.

Carbon 14 and the Prehistory of Europe

3

by Colin Renfrew
October 1971

Tree-ring measurements have shown that early carbon-14 dates are off by as much as 700 years. As a result the view that cultural advances diffused into Europe from the east is no longer tenable

Our knowledge of European prehistory is currently being revolutionized. The immediate cause of the revolution is a recently discovered discrepancy between the actual ages of many archaeological sites and the ages that have been attributed to them on the basis of carbon-14 analysis. Some sites are as much as seven centuries older than they had been thought to be. This revelation has destroyed the intricate system of interlocking chronologies that provided the foundation for a major edifice of archaeological scholarship: the theory of cultural diffusion.

For more than a century a basic assumption of prehistorians has been that most of the major cultural advances in ancient Europe came about as the result of influences from the great early civilizations of Egypt and Mesopotamia. For example, megalithic tombs in western Europe feature single slabs that weigh several tons. The prevailing view of their origin was that the technical skills and religious motivation needed for their construction had come from the eastern Mediterranean, first reaching Spain and Portugal and then France, Britain and Scandinavia. To take another example, it was generally supposed that the knowledge of copper metallurgy had been transmitted by Mediterranean intermediaries to the Iberian peninsula and to the Balkans from its place of origin in the Near East. The revolution in chronology shows, however, that the megalithic tombs of western Europe and the copper metallurgy of the Balkans are actually older than their supposed Mediterranean prototypes.

When the scholars of a century ago wanted to date the monuments and objects of prehistoric Europe, they had little to help them. C. J. Thomsen, a Danish student of antiquities, had established a "three ages" frame of reference in 1836; structures and objects were roughly classified as Stone Age (at first there was no distinction between Paleolithic and Neolithic), Bronze Age or Iron Age. To assign such things an age in years was a matter of little more than guesswork.

Prehistoric finds are of course by their nature unaccompanied by written records. The only possible recourse was to work from the known to the unknown: to try to move outward toward the unlettered periphery from the historical civilizations of Egypt and Mesopotamia, where written records were available. For example, the historical chronology of Egypt, based on ancient written records, can be extended with considerable confidence back to 1900 B.C. because

MEGALITHIC MONUMENT near Essé in Brittany is typical of the massive stone structures that were raised in France as long ago as the fifth millennium B.C. Called "Fairies' Rock," it is made of 42 large slabs of schist, some weighing more than 40 tons. Because of the great effort that must have been required to raise such monuments, scholars traditionally refused to credit the barbarian cultures of prehistoric Europe with their construction and instead attributed them to influences from civilized eastern Mediterranean.

the records noted astronomical events. The Egyptian "king lists" can then be used, although with far less confidence, to build up a chronology that goes back another 11 centuries to 3000 B.C.

The need to establish a link with Egypt in order to date the prehistoric cultures of Europe went naturally with the widespread assumption that, among prehistoric sites in general, the more sophisticated ones were of Near Eastern origin anyway. In 1887, when the brothers Henri and Louis Siret published the results of their excavations in the cemeteries and settlements of "Copper Age" (late Neolithic) Spain, they reported finding stone tombs, some roofed with handsome corbeled stonework and others of massive megalithic construction. In the tombs there were sometimes human figurines carved in stone, and daggers and simple tools made of copper. That these structures and objects had evolved locally did not seem likely; an origin in the eastern Mediterranean—in Egypt or the Aegean—was claimed for all their more exotic features.

In the first years of this century this method of building up relationships and using contacts with the early civilized world to establish a relative chronology was put on a systematic basis by the Swedish archaeologist Oskar Montelius. In 1903 Montelius published an account of his "typological method," where the development of particular types of tools or weapons within a given area was reconstructed and the sequence was then compared with those of neighboring areas. Adjacent regions could thus be linked in a systematic manner, until a chain of links was built up stretching from the Atlantic across Europe to Egypt and Mesopotamia. It was still assumed that most of the innovations had come from the Near East, and that the farther from the "hearthlands" of civilization they were found, the longer it would have taken them to diffuse there.

Some diffusionist scholars went to extremes. In the 1920's Sir Grafton Smith argued the view that nearly all the innovations in the civilizations around the world could be traced back to Egypt. In this hyperdiffusionist theory the high cultures of the Far East and even the early civilizations of Central America and South America had supposedly stemmed from Egypt. Today very few continue to suppose that the essential ingredients of civilization were disseminated from Egypt to the rest of the world, perhaps in papyrus boats. There were, of course, scholars whose views lay at the other extreme, such as the German ultranationalist Gustaf Kossinna, whose chauvinist writings fell into a predictable pattern. For these men the truly great advances and fundamental discoveries always seem to have been made in the land of their birth. The *Herrenvolk* fantasies of Aryan supremacy in the Nazi era were rooted in Kossinna's theory of Nordic primacy.

Appalled by both of these extremes, the British prehistorian V. Gordon Childe tried to steer a middle course. In *The Dawn of European Civilisation*, published in 1925, Childe rejected Smith's fantasy that the ancient Egyptians were responsible for all the significant advances in prehistoric Europe. Working in the same framework as Montelius but with a detailed and sympathetic consideration of the prehistoric cultures of each region, he built up a picture in terms of what one colleague, Glyn E. Daniel, has termed "modified diffusionism."

Childe saw two main paths whereby a chronological link could be established between Europe and the Near East. First there were the Spanish "Copper Age" finds. Earlier writers had likened the megalithic tombs of Spain, particularly those with corbeled vaults, to the great tholos tombs of Mycenae, which were built around 1500 B.C. Childe saw that the Mycenaean tombs were too recent to have served as a model, and he suggested instead a link between the Spanish tombs and the round tombs of Bronze Age Crete, which had been built

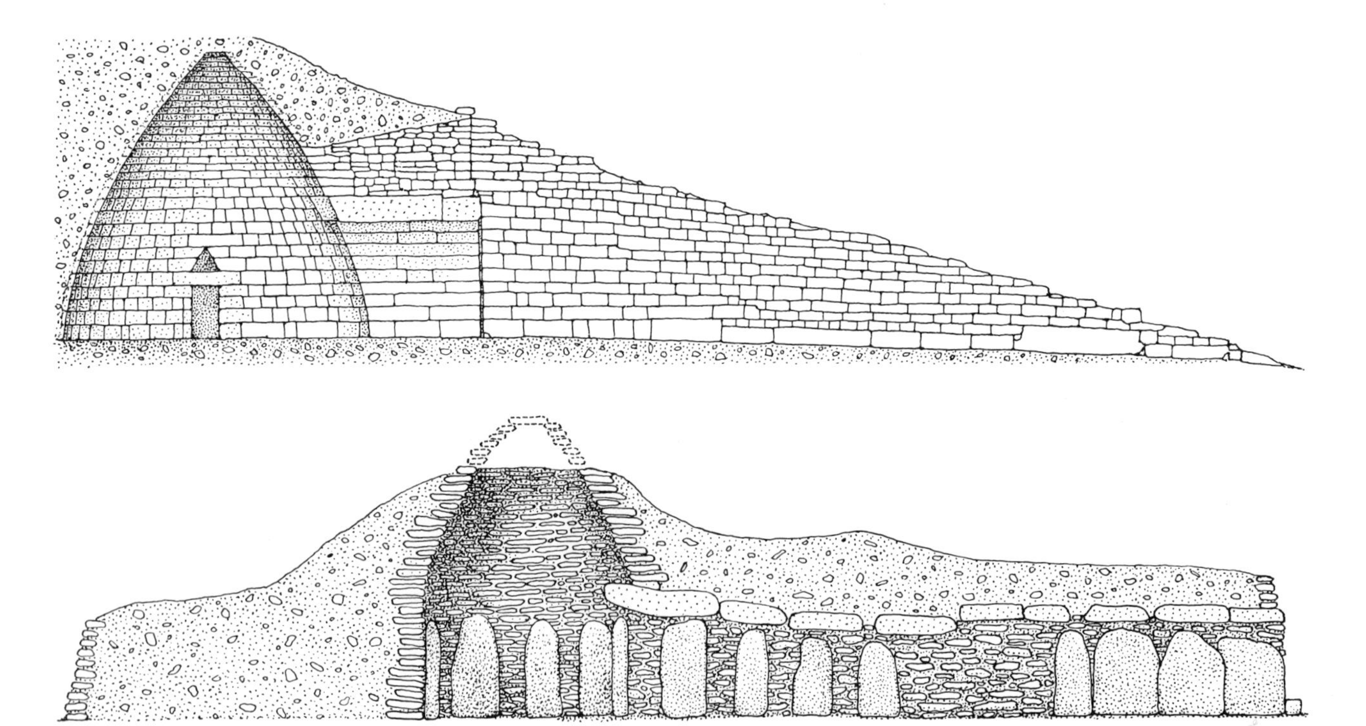

TWO SIMILAR STRUCTURES with corbeled domes are the famous "Treasury of Atreus," a Mycenaean tomb built around 1500 B.C. (*top*), and a megalithic passage grave, Île Longue in Brittany, which is probably some 6,000 years old (*bottom*). Unaware of the true age of the French passage graves, the prehistorian V. Gordon Childe nonetheless dismissed the notion that they were inspired by a civilization as recent as Mycenae. He suggested that they were probably modeled on earlier Minoan tombs built around 2500 B.C.

about 2500 B.C. As subsequent work provided more detail, it was even suggested that colonists from the Aegean had set up settlements in Spain and Portugal. With them they would have brought their knowledge of architecture, their custom of collective burial, their belief in a "mother goddess" and their skill in metallurgy. The fortifications at one or two of these early Iberian sites resemble those at the settlement of Chalandriani on the Aegean island of Syros [*see bottom illustration at right*].

It was on this basis that the earliest megalithic tombs of the Iberian peninsula were assigned an age of around 2500 B.C. The similar French and British tombs, some of which also have stone vaults, were assigned to times a little later in the third millennium.

Similar logic was used in assigning dates to the striking stone temples of Malta. Sculptured slabs in some of the island's temples are handsomely decorated with spirals. These spirals resemble decorations from Crete and Greece of the period from 1800 to 1600 B.C. The Maltese temples were therefore assumed to date from that time or a little later.

Childe's second path for chronological links between western Europe and the Near East was the Danube. Artifacts of the late Neolithic period found at Vinča in Yugoslavia were compared by him to material from the early Bronze Age "cities" at Troy. The Trojan finds can be dated to within a few centuries of 2700 B.C. It was concluded that metallurgy had arisen in the Balkans as a result of contacts with Troy. This view was strengthened by certain similarities between the clay sculptures found at Vinča and various artistic products of the early Bronze Age Aegean.

These twin foundations for the prehistoric chronology of Europe have been accepted by most archaeologists since Childe's day. The appearance of metallurgy and of other striking cultural and artistic abilities in the Balkans, and of monumental architecture on the Iberian peninsula, were explained as the result of contacts with the Aegean. Such skills make their appearance in the Aegean around 2500 B.C., a point in time that is established by finds of datable Egyptian imports in Crete and of somewhat later Cretan exports in datable contexts in Egypt. The chronology of Crete and the southern Aegean is soundly based on the chronology of Egypt and has not been affected by the current revolution.

It should be noted that, as Childe himself pointed out, these conclusions rested on two basic assumptions. First, it

TWO SIMILAR SPIRALS are the decorations on a stele from a Mycenaean shaft grave (*top*) and decorations at temple of Tarxien in Malta (*bottom*). Mycenaean spirals were carved about 1650 B.C. Maltese ones were held on grounds of resemblance to be same age.

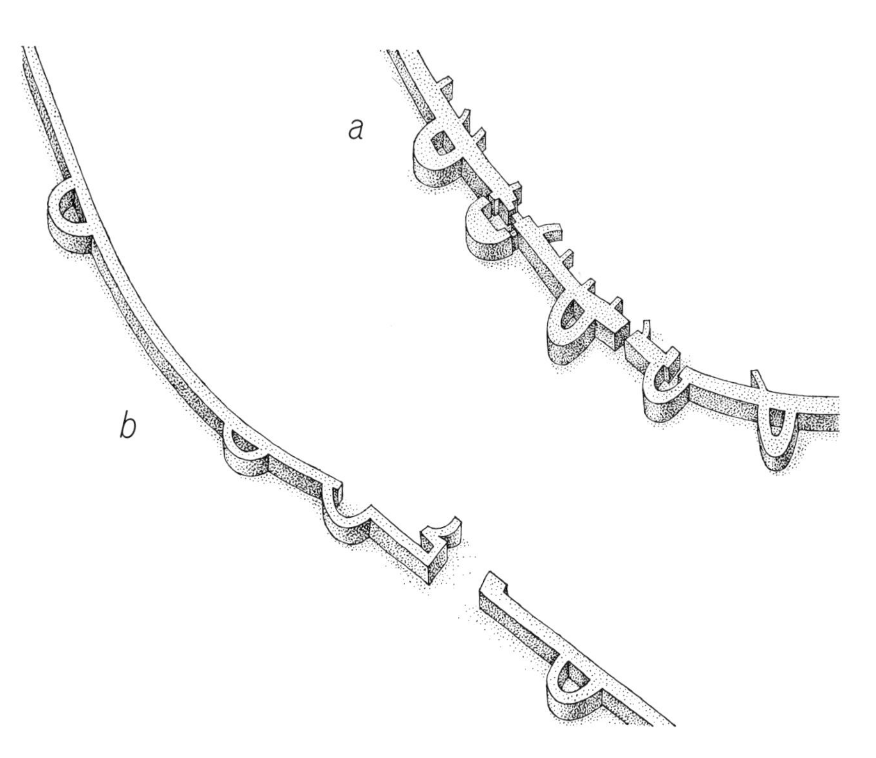

TWO SIMILAR FORTIFICATIONS are the bastioned walls at Chalandriani (*a*), a site on the Aegean island of Syros, and the walls of Los Millares (*b*), a "Copper Age" site near Málaga in Spain. The likeness was once attributed to the work of Aegean colonists in Spain.

was assumed that "parallel" developments in different regions—the appearance of metallurgy or the beginning of monumental tomb architecture—were not entirely independent innovations. Second, it was assumed that if the developments had indeed diffused from one region to another, the ancient civilizations of the Near East were the innovators and the barbarians of Europe were the beneficiaries. Childe realized that these assumptions could be questioned, but in the absence of any independent dating method the only way prehistoric Europe could be dated at all was to relate it to the dated civilizations of the Near East. In practice this meant full acceptance of the assumptions. As Childe remarked of his work, "the sole unifying theme was the irradiation of European barbarism by Oriental civilization."

The discovery of carbon-14 dating in 1949 offered, in principle at least, the possibility of establishing a sound absolute chronology without the need for the assumptions that Childe had had to make. Even without carbon-14 dating, however, some of the arguments of the modified diffusionist school were susceptible to criticism. For example, there are no megalithic tombs in the Aegean, so that some special pleading is needed to argue a Near Eastern origin for those of western Europe. Again, detailed studies in the Aegean area show that the resemblances between the pottery and figurines of the Iberian peninsula and those of Greece, the supposed homeland of the "colonists," are not as close as had been supposed. Nor are the Balkan Neolithic finds really very closely related to the Aegean ones from which they were supposedly derived. There was certainly room for doubt about some of the details in the attractive and coherent picture that diffusionist theory had built up.

Although the introduction of carbon-14 dating did not disrupt the diffusionist picture or the chronology based on it, the dates did produce a few anomalies. A decade ago there were already hints that something was wrong. The carbon-14 method, originated by Willard F. Libby, ingeniously exploits the production of atoms of this heavy isotope of carbon in the upper atmosphere. The carbon-14 atoms are produced by the absorption of neutrons by atoms of nitrogen 14. The neutrons in turn are produced by the impact of cosmic ray particles on various atoms in the atmosphere. Carbon 14 is radioactive, and like all radioactive elements it decays in a regular way. Its half-life was originally estimated by Libby to be some 5,568 years.

The manufacture of the radioactive isotope by cosmic radiation and its diminution through decay sets up a balance so that the proportion of carbon 14 to carbon 12, the much more abundant nonradioactive isotope, is approximately constant. The atoms of the radioactive isotope in the atmosphere, like the atoms of normal carbon, combine with oxygen to form carbon dioxide. This substance is taken up by plants through photosynthesis and by animals feeding on the plants, and in that way all living things come to have the two kinds of carbon in the same proportion in their tissues while they are alive. At death, however, the cycle is broken: the organisms no longer take up any fresh carbon and the proportion of the two isotopes steadily changes as the radioactive isotope decays. Assuming that the proportion of the two isotopes in the atmosphere has always been constant, one can measure how much carbon 14 is left in plant or animal remains (in charcoal, say, or bone) and, knowing the half-life of the radioactive isotope, can calculate how long the decay process has been going on and therefore how old the sample is.

This, put rather simply, is the principle of the dating method. In practice it is complicated by the very small number of carbon-14 atoms in the atmosphere and in living things compared with the number of carbon-12 atoms: approximately one per million million. The proportion is of course further reduced in dead organic material as the rare isotope decays, making accurate measurement a delicate task. Nonetheless, samples from archaeological sites began to yield coherent and consistent dates soon after 1949. In general the carbon-14 dates in Europe tallied fairly well with those built up by the "typological method"

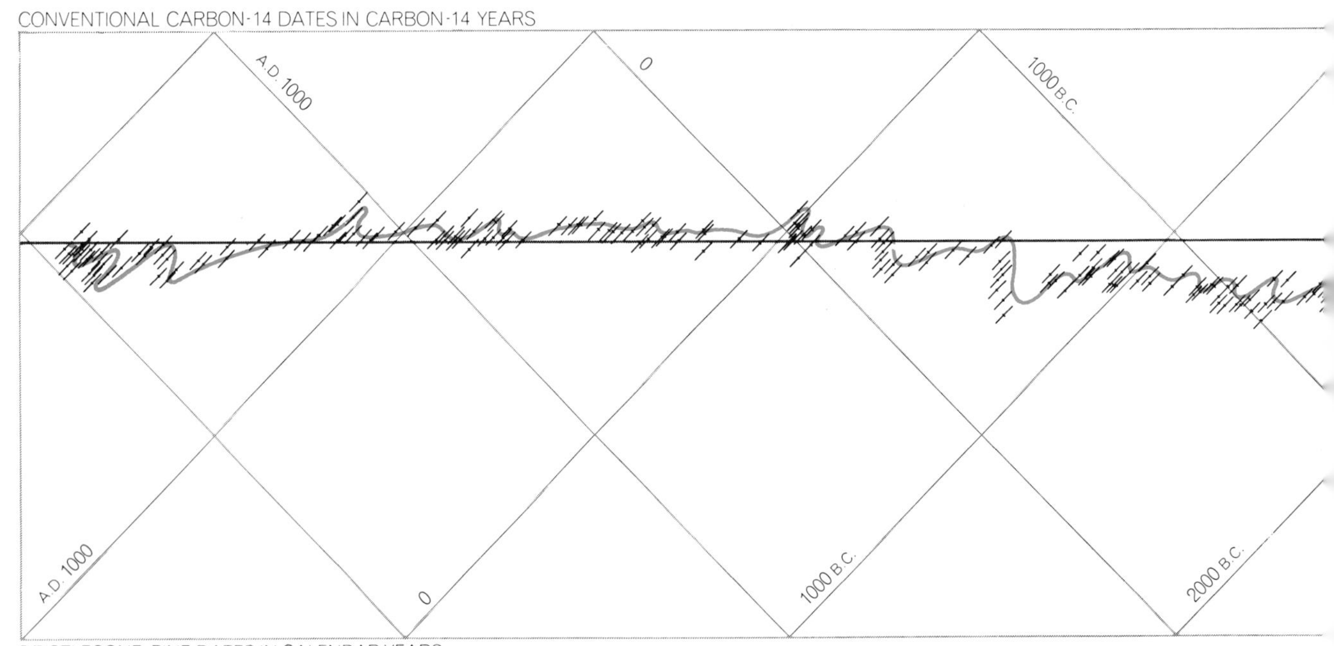

BRISTLECONE-PINE CALIBRATION worked out by Hans E. Suess of the University of California at San Diego makes it possible to correct carbon-14 dates. The dates running across the top and the lines on which they rest refer to carbon-14 dates in carbon-14 years; the dates running across the bottom and the lines on which they rest refer to bristlecone-pine dates in calendar years. The colback to about 2500 B.C. The great surprise was how early the Neolithic period, defined by the appearance of farming villages, began everywhere. Instead of yielding the expected dates of around 4000 or 4500 B.C., the earliest villages in the Near East proved to date back to as early as 8000 B.C.

These dates for the early Neolithic period were most important. Indeed, their impact on prehistoric archaeology can be regarded as the first carbon-14 revolution. The sharp increases in age did not, however, actually disrupt the diffusionist picture. Farming developments in the Near East remained in general earlier than those in Europe. The pattern did not change nor did the Near East lose its primacy; it was just that all the dates were earlier than had been expected. Everyone had always been aware that, for the period before 3000 B.C., which is when the Egyptian chronology begins, all dates were guesswork. What the first carbon-14 dates demonstrated was that the guesses had not been bold enough.

Thus the first carbon-14 revolution did not seriously challenge the relationships that had previously been established in terms of relative chronology between the different areas of Europe and the Near East. Even with respect to the crucial period after 3000 B.C., for which the Egyptian historical chronology provided a framework of absolute rather than relative dating, the new dates seemed to harmonize fairly well with the traditional ones. Just three troublesome problems hinted that all was not yet well. First, whereas many of the early carbon-14 dates for the megalithic tombs in western Europe fell around 2500 B.C., which fitted in with Childe's traditional chronology, the dates in France were somewhat earlier. In Brittany, for example, the dates of several corbeled tombs were earlier than 3000 B.C. This did not agree with the established picture of megalithic tombs diffusing from Spain to France sometime after 2500 B.C. Most scholars simply assumed that the French laboratories producing these dates were no better than they ought to be, and that the anomaly would probably disappear when more dates were available.

Second, the dates for the Balkan Neolithic were far too early. Sites related to the Vinča culture gave carbon-14 readings as early as 4000 B.C. This implied that not only copper metallurgy but also the attractive little sculptures of the Balkans were more than a millennium older than their supposed Aegean prototypes. Clearly something was wrong. Some archaeologists, led by Vladimir Milojčić, argued that the entire carbon-14 method was in error. Others felt that some special factor was making the Balkan dates too early, since the dates in other regions, with the exception of Brittany, seemed to be in harmony with the historical dates for the third millennium B.C.

Third, the dates for Egypt were too late. In retrospect this now seems highly significant. Egyptian objects historically dated to the period between 3000 and 2000 B.C. consistently yielded carbon-14 dates that placed them several centuries later. With the early inaccuracies and uncertainties of the carbon-14 method these divergences could at first be dismissed as random errors, but as more dates accumulated such an excuse was no longer possible. The archaeologists kept on using their historical dates and did not bother too much about the problems raised by the new method.

The physicists were more concerned, but they supposed, to use Libby's words, "that the Egyptian historical dates beyond 4000 years ago may be somewhat too old, perhaps five centuries too old at 5000 years ago, with decrease in error to [zero] at 4000 years ago.... It is noteworthy that the earliest astronomical fix is at 4000 years ago, that all older dates have errors and that these errors are more or less cumulative with time before 4000 years ago." For once, however, the archaeologists were right. The discrepancy was to be set at the door of the physicist rather than the Egyptologist. The consequences were dramatic.

Remote as it may seem from European archaeology, it was the venerable pine trees in the White Mountains of

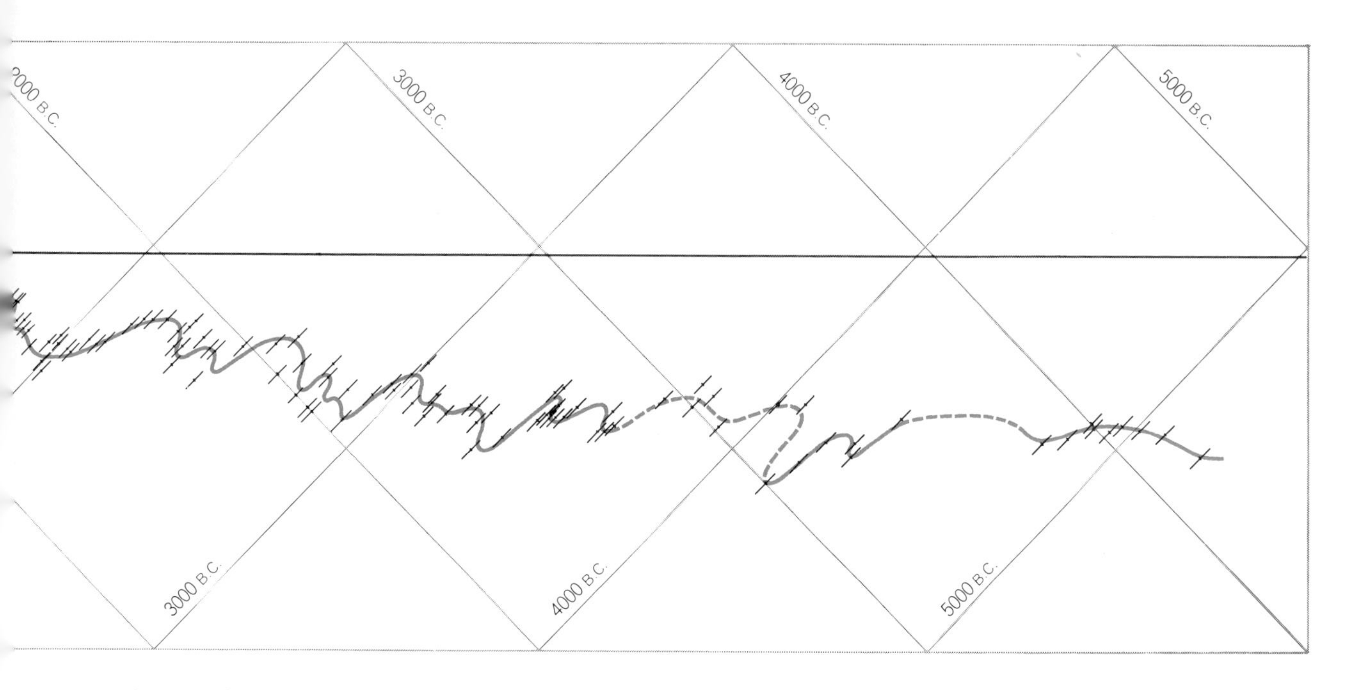

ored curve, which follows many individual measurements, shows how the carbon-14 dates go off with time. To calibrate a carbon-14 date, say 2000 B.C., one follows the line for that date until it meets the colored curve. At that point a diagonal is drawn parallel to the bristlecone-pine lines and the date is read off on the bristlecone-pine scale. The corrected date would be about 2500 B.C.

YEARS B.C.	EGYPT	AEGEAN	BALKANS	ITALY	MALTA
1500	DYNASTY XVIII	MYCENAE			
1500–2000		MIDDLE BRONZE AGE	FÜZESABONY	POLADA	TARXIEN CEMETE
2000–2500		EARLY BRONZE AGE	NAGYREV		
2500	PYRAMIDS	LERNA III			TARXIEN
2500–3000		TROY I		REMEDELLO	
3000–3500	DYNASTY I	EARLY HELLADIC I			GGANTIJA
3500–4000	GERZEAN	FINAL NEOLITHIC	LATE GUMELNITSA	LAGOZZA	ZEBBUG
4000–4500	AMRATIAN	LATE NEOLITHIC	LATE VINČA	CHIOZZA	RED SKORBA
4500			EARLY VINČA		

REVISED CHRONOLOGY, taking the Suess calibration into account, destroys the basis for the diffusionist theory of European prehistory. Colored area at left marks the portion of Egyptian and Aegean chronology that is related to historical records. Colored

California that brought about the revolution in Old World prehistory. These trees have provided a reliable check of the carbon-14 method and have produced significant modifications. By 1960 one major assumption of the method was already coming into question. This was that the rate of production of carbon 14 in the atmosphere, and hence its proportion in all living things, had been constant over the past 40,000 years. The assumption was first really checked when Eric H. Willis, Henrik Tauber and Karl Otto Münnich analyzed samples of wood from the stump of a giant sequoia that could be dated exactly by counting its annual growth rings. Although the carbon-14 dates and the tree-ring dates agreed to within 100 years all the way back to A.D. 650, some minor but real fluctuations were observed. This suggested that there had been definite small changes in the rate of carbon-14 production in the past.

It was obviously desirable to check back to even earlier periods. Fortunately the fantastically long life of the California bristlecone pine (*Pinus aristata*) was known to the late Edmund Schulman of the Laboratory of Tree-Ring Research at the University of Arizona. Bristlecone pines as old as 4,600 years had been authenticated. Since Schulman's death the study of the trees has been energetically pursued by Charles Wesley Ferguson of the same laboratory. With ring sequences from many bristlecones, Ferguson has succeeded in building up a continuous absolute chronology reaching back nearly 8,200 years. The compilation of such a chronology, with due provision for multiple growth rings and missing rings, is a formidable task. Ferguson and his colleagues have developed computer programs for the comparison and matching of the ring sequence of different trees. This admirably systematic work has been the indispensable foundation of the second carbon-14 revolution.

Ferguson supplied wood samples whose absolute age had been determined by ring-counting to three independent carbon-14 laboratories: one at the University of Arizona, one at the University of Pennsylvania and one at the University of California at San Diego. The carbon-14 determinations, which in general agree fairly well with one another, reveal major discrepancies between previously accepted carbon-14 dates and actual dates. At San Diego, Hans E. Suess has analyzed more than 300 such samples and has built up an impressively clear and coherent picture of these discrepancies.

The divergence between the carbon-14 and tree-ring dates is not serious after 1500 B.C. Before that time the difference becomes progressively larger and amounts to as much as 700 years by 2500 B.C. The carbon-14 dates are all too young, but Suess's analysis can be used to correct them [*see illustration on preceding two pages*].

One problem that has emerged is that, in addition to a large first-order divergence, Suess's calibration curve shows smaller second-order fluctuations or "kinks." Sometimes the rate of carbon-14 production has fluctuated so rapidly that samples of different ages show an identical concentration of carbon 14 in spite of the fact that the older sample allowed more time for radioactive decay. This means that a given carbon-14 date can very well correspond to several different calendar dates.

The reasons for the fluctuations are not yet known with certainty, but the Czechoslovakian geophysicist V. Bucha has shown that there is a striking correlation between the divergence in dates and past changes in the strength of the earth's magnetic field. The first-order variation is probably due to the fact that as the strength of the earth's field changed it deflected more or fewer cosmic rays before they could enter the atmosphere. There are strong indications that the second-order fluctuations are correlated with the level of solar activity. Both the low-energy particles of the "solar wind" and the high-energy particles that are the solar component of the cosmic radiation may affect the cosmic ray flux in the vicinity of the earth. Climatic changes may also have influenced the concentration of carbon 14 in the atmosphere.

To the archaeologist, however, the reliability of the tree-ring calibration is more important than its physical basis. Libby's principle of simultaneity, which states that the atmospheric level of carbon 14 at a given time is uniform all

IBERIA	FRANCE	BRITISH ISLES	NORTH EUROPE
EL ARGAR		MIDDLE BRONZE AGE	BRONZE HORIZON III
	EARLY BRONZE AGE	STONEHENGE III	HORIZON II
BEAKER	BEAKER		HORIZON I
	SEINE-OISE-MARNE CULTURE	STONEHENGE I	MIDDLE NEOLITHIC (PASSAGE GRAVES)
LOS MILLARES		NEW GRANGE	
ALMERIAN	LATE PASSAGE GRAVE	NEOLITHIC	TRICHTERBECKER "A"
ARLY ALMERIAN			ERTEBØLLE
	EARLY CHASSEY	EARLY NEOLITHIC	

area at right indicates periods when megalithic monuments were built in the European areas named. Lines and names in color show "connections" now proved to be impossible.

over the world, has been in large measure substantiated. Tests of nuclear weapons have shown that atmospheric mixing is rapid and that irregularities in composition are smoothed out after a few years. The California calibration should therefore hold for Europe. There is no need to assume that tree growth or tree rings are similar on the two continents, only that the atmospheric level of carbon 14 is the same at a given time.

There remains the question of whether some special factor in the bristlecone pine itself might be causing the discrepancies. For example, the diffusion of recent sap across the old tree rings and its retention in them might affect the reading if the sap were not removed by laboratory cleaning procedures. Studies are now in progress to determine if this is a significant factor; present indications are that it is not. Even if it is, it would be difficult to see why the discrepancy between carbon-14 dates and calendar dates should be large only before 1500 B.C.

The general opinion, as reflected in the discussions at the Twelfth Nobel Symposium at Uppsala in 1969, is that the discrepancy is real. Suess's calibration curve is the best now available, although corrections and modifications can be expected. It is particularly satisfying that when the carbon-14 dates for Egypt are calibrated, they agree far better with the Egyptian historical calendar. Further work is now in progress at the University of California at Los Angeles and at the British Museum on Egyptian samples specially collected for the project, so that a further check of the extent to which the calibrated carbon-14 dates and the historical chronology are in harmony will soon be available.

The revision of carbon-14 dates for prehistoric Europe has a disastrous effect on the traditional diffusionist chronology. The significant point is not so much that the European dates in the third millennium are all several centuries earlier than was supposed but that the dates for Egypt do not change. Prehistorians have always used the historical dates for Egypt because they seemed more accurate than the carbon-14 dates. They have been proved correct; the calibrated carbon-14 dates for Egypt agree far better with the historical chronology than the uncalibrated ones did. Hence the Egyptian historical calendar, and with it the conventional Egyptian chronology, remains unchanged. The same is true for the Near East in general and for Crete and the southern Aegean. The carbon-14 dates for the Aegean formerly seemed too young; they too agree better after calibration.

For the rest of Europe this is not true. Over the past decade prehistorians in Europe have increasingly been using carbon-14 dates to build up a chronology of the third millennium B.C. Except in Brittany and the Balkans, this chronology had seemed to work fairly well. The dates had still allowed the megalithic tombs of Spain to have been built around 2500 B.C. There was no direct contradiction between the diffusionist picture and the uncalibrated carbon-14 chronology.

All that is now changed. A carbon-14 date of about 2350 B.C. for the walls and tombs at Los Millares in Spain must now be set around 2900 B.C. This makes the structures older than their supposed prototypes in the Aegean. Whereas the carbon-14 inconsistency in western Europe was formerly limited to Brittany, it now applies to the entire area. In almost every region where megalithic tombs are found the calibrated carbon-14 dates substantially predate 2500 B.C. The view of megalithic culture as an import from the Near East no longer works.

The same thing seems to be happening in Malta, although there are still too few carbon-14 dates to be certain. A date of 1930 B.C. for the period *after* the temples now becomes about 2200 B.C. Clearly the spirals in the temples cannot be the result of Aegean influence around 1800 B.C.

The Balkans are affected too. The figurines of the Vinča culture now have dates earlier than 4500 B.C.; to associate them with the Aegean of the third millennium becomes ludicrous. The revision of dates also shows that in the Balkans there was a flourishing tradition of copper metallurgy, including such useful artifacts as tools with shaft holes, before metal production was well under way in the Aegean.

Similar changes are seen all over Europe. Stonehenge was until recently considered by many to be the work of skilled craftsmen or architects who had come to Britain from Mycenaean Greece around 1500 B.C. The monument is now seen to be several centuries older, and Mycenaean influence is clearly out of the question.

All is not confusion, however. As we have seen, the chronology of Egypt, the Near East, Crete and the Aegean is not materially changed in the third millennium B.C. Although the actual dates are altered in the rest of Europe, when we compare areas dated solely by carbon 14 the relationships between them are not changed. The great hiatus comes when we compare areas that have calibrated carbon-14 dates with areas that are dated by historical means. The hiatus may be likened to a geological fault; the chronological "fault line" extends across the Mediterranean and southern Europe.

On each side of the fault line the relationships and the successions of cultures remain unaltered. The two sides have shifted, however, *en bloc* in relation to each other, as the geological stra-

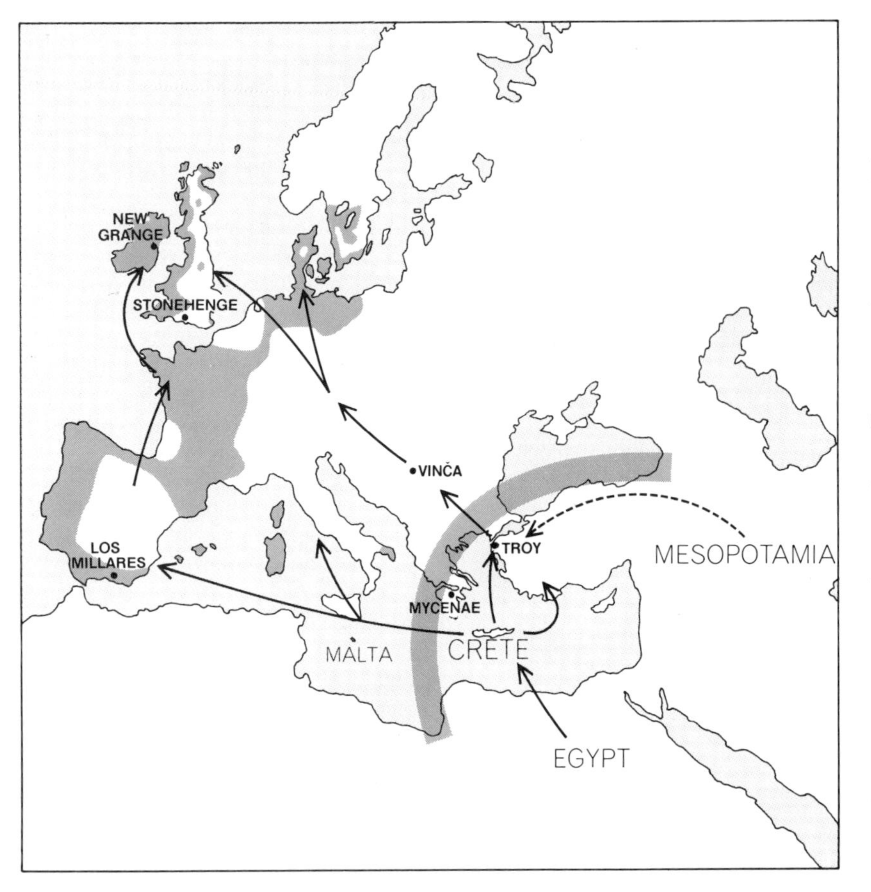

CHRONOLOGICAL "FAULT LINE" *(curved bar)* **divides all Europe except the Aegean from the Near East. Arrows above the fault line are supposed chronological links now discredited. Areas of Europe that contain megalithic chamber tombs are in color at left.**

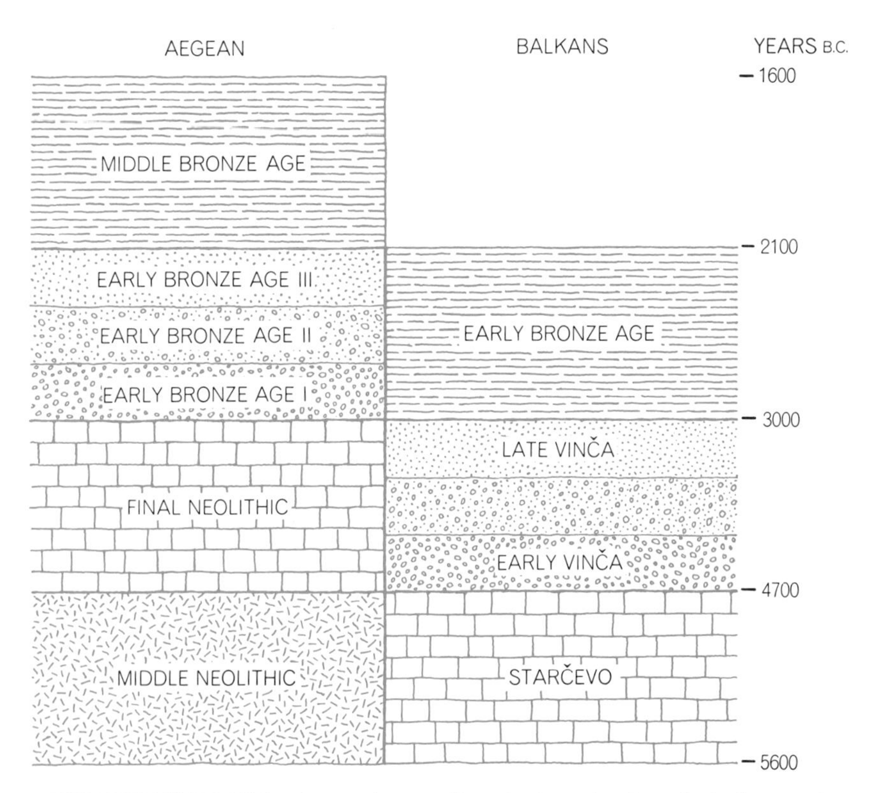

FAULT-LINE SLIPPAGE is shown schematically as it affects the chronological connection between the barbarian Balkans and the civilized Aegean. Strata with the same markings were once thought to be contemporary. Estimated Balkan dates, however, were too recent.

ta on two sides of a fault might. As a result much of what Montelius and Childe wrote about relationships and relative chronologies within continental Europe still stands. It is only the absolute chronology in calendar years and certain key links—between Spain and the Aegean and between the Balkans and the Aegean—that are ruptured. The dates for Europe as a whole have moved back in time, and the old diffusionist view of links connecting Europe and the Near East is no longer tenable.

The really important effect of tree-ring calibration is not that it changes the dates for prehistoric Europe by a few centuries. What matters is that it transforms our picture of what happened in prehistoric Europe and of how Europe developed. No longer can the essential theme of European prehistory be Childe's "irradiation of European barbarism by Oriental civilization." Indeed, the very early dates for some of the achievements of the prehistoric inhabitants of Europe make the term barbarism quite inappropriate.

Now it is clear that megalithic chamber tombs were being built in Brittany earlier than 4000 B.C., a millennium before monumental funerary architecture first appears in the eastern Mediterranean and 1,500 years before the raising of the pyramids. The origins of these European burial customs and monuments have to be sought not in the Near East but in Europe itself. The temples of Malta must likewise be viewed as remarkable, indeed unique, local creations: the oldest freestanding stone monuments in the world.

Even metallurgy may have been independently invented in the Balkans, and possibly in Spain as well. Certainly it was flourishing in the Balkans earlier than it was in Greece. The possibility remains, however, that the art of metalworking was learned from the Near East, where it was known even earlier than in the Balkans.

The central moral is inescapable. In the past we have completely undervalued the originality and the creativity of the inhabitants of prehistoric Europe. It was a mistake, as we now can see, always to seek in the Near East an explanation for the changes taking place in Europe. Diffusion has been overplayed. Of course, contact between prehistoric cultures often allowed ideas and innovations to pass between them. Furthermore, evidence might easily emerge for occasional contacts between western or southern Europe and the Near East in very early times. This, however, is not an adequate model for the explanation of culture change. Nor is there any case for turning the tables on the old diffusionists by suggesting that the early monuments and innovations in Europe inspired the pyramids of Egypt or other achievements in the Near East. That would merely be to reverse the arrows on the diffusionist map, and to miss the real lesson of the new dating.

The initial impact of the carbon-14 revolution will be to lead archaeologists to revise their dates for prehistoric Europe. This is the basic factual contribution that the tree-ring calibration has to make, although inevitably it will be some years before we can develop a definitive and reliable calibrated chronology for the entire area. The more profound impact, however, will be on the kind of explanation that prehistorians will accept in elucidating cultural change. A greater reluctance to swallow "influences" or "contacts" as sufficient explanations in themselves, without a much more detailed analysis of the actual mechanisms involved, is to be expected. This is in keeping with much current archaeological thinking. Today social and economic processes are increasingly seen as more important subjects for study than the similarities among artifacts.

When the textbooks are rewritten, as they will have to be, it is not only the European dates that will be altered. A shift in the basic nature of archaeological reasoning is necessary. Indeed, it is already taking place in Europe and in other parts of the world. This is the key change that tree-ring calibration, however uncertain some of its details remain, has helped to bring about.

ANCIENT PINE, its trunk scarred and its branches twisted, is one of the many trees of the bristlecone species (*Pinus aristata*) that grow in the White Mountains of California. An analysis of this tree's growth rings proves it to be more than 4,500 years old. Using this and other specimens, Charles Wesley Ferguson and his co-workers at the University of Arizona have built up a continuous tree-ring chronology with a span of more than 8,000 years.

4

Megalithic Monuments

by Glyn Daniel
July 1980

These assemblages of massive stones, of which Stonehenge is one, are found by the thousands in Europe. How old they are was long uncertain, but they have now been dated to the Neolithic period

Among the most dramatic remains of the ancient cultural landscape of Europe are its many prehistoric stone monuments. These megaliths have long aroused the interest and curiosity both of the general public and of antiquarians and archaeologists, with their interest in correctly describing the nature, purpose, context and age of the structures. To give only two examples, the stone rows of the Carnac region in southern Brittany, where more than 3,000 menhirs stand in parallel lines that extend for nearly four miles, and the Grand Menhir Brisé at nearby Locmariaquer, now broken but originally 22 meters long, are among the most remarkable relics of prehistoric France.

Without doubt the most famous of all megalithic monuments is Stonehenge, on the Wiltshire plain of southern Britain. Visited by thousands yearly, it is second only to the Tower of London as a tourist attraction. It has a larger literature than any other archaeological site in the world, including the pyramids of Egypt and the great statues of Easter Island, as well as mythical sites such as Atlantis. The number of books on Stonehenge and on other megalithic monuments that have poured from the presses in the past decade or so is a measure of the continued interest in these antiquities.

It is also, alas, an all too clear demonstration of the imagination, wishful thinking and credulousness of many authors, and the abysmal ignorance of many alleged archaeologists who can only be described, if uncharitably, as fantasy buffs. This is no new phenomenon. As long ago as 1911 G. Elliot Smith's book *The Ancient Egyptians* brought all these ancient European monuments from the banks of the Nile. Such exercises of the imagination continue. As recently as 1977 Euan MacKie in *The Megalith Builders* declared that they were the work of wise men from predynastic Egypt and Sumeria. There are others, among them Erich von Däniken, who see the megalith builders as voyagers from space. Now there is also a widespread belief that these monuments were built with an astronomical purpose, and such words as "astro-archaeology" and "archaeoastronomy" are freely bandied about. Let us take a sober and balanced look at these structures in the context of our existing detailed knowledge of ancient Europe.

The Study of Megaliths

In 1849 in a book called *Cyclops Christianus* an Oxford don, Algernon Herbert, coined the word megalith (from the Greek *megas,* great, and *lithos,* stone). The word caught on. Although in 1872 James Fergusson, a Scottish architectural scholar, titled his book *Rude Stone Monuments in All Countries,* he too spoke of megaliths. So did T. E. Peet in his *Rough Stone Monuments,* published 40 years later.

These pioneer works established the proper study of megaliths, but they introduced one fundamental confusion. As travelers such as Fergusson journeyed outside Europe they found great stone monuments in Algeria, Palestine, Ethiopia and the Sudan, the Caucasus, Persia, Baluchistan, Kashmir and central and southern India. (In India the megalithic monuments of the Deccan, many of them with "portholes" resembling those of megalithic tombs in Europe, first interested Fergusson in undertaking his comparative researches.) The list does not end there. Megaliths are found in Assam, in Sumatra and on some Pacific islands such as Malekula in the New Hebrides. (The stone figures of Easter Island, although they are certainly large, are not megaliths in the generally accepted sense.) In Japan megalithic tombs were built from the second century B.C. until the seventh century A.D., when the emperor Kotoku forbade them as a waste of labor. The pre-Columbian civilizations of the New World also practiced megalithic construction.

The result of applying the term megalith to all these monuments in different countries, from different periods and in different cultural contexts gave birth to an absurdity: the idea that the structures were genetically connected, that they were the work of a megalithic race or a megalithic people. This notion has long been abandoned, and it is widely realized that the megalithic structures in different parts of the world are similar because they are made of similar materials in similar ways. The parallels are particularly striking in megalithic chambers or rooms that incorporate the basic elements of what is known as trabeate architecture (from the Latin *trabes,* beam). This type of construction is like building a house of cards or of children's blocks: slabs of stone are set upright (orthostats) and other slabs are laid across the uprights as capstones. The architectural possibilities are limited, and so it is not surprising that a megalithic chamber in France or Ireland, dating from the third millennium B.C., should resemble a megalithic chamber in southern India dating from the end of the first millennium B.C.

Another confusion in the minds of many is one between megalithic architecture and cyclopean architecture. The latter also makes use of large stones, but a cyclopean structure is built of stones that are carefully fitted together, even if irregular in shape, and generally set in layers. Cyclopean architecture is found in both the New World (for example the Inca structures of Peru) and the Old (for example the citadels of Mycenae and Tiryns in Greece or the nuraghi, or stone towers, of Sardinia).

The European Megaliths

The megalithic structures of Europe fall into four main categories. First is the menhir, or single standing stone. The word comes from the Welsh *maen,* a stone, and *hir,* long. Brittany is rich in menhirs that range in length from one meter to six meters. A notable exception is the Grand Menhir Brisé, a much larger horizontal stone. No one knows whether this great stone ever stood erect; the earliest records describe it as it is now.

A special kind of menhir, known as a statue menhir, is sculptured so that it bears the representation of a person, hu-

GRAND ARRAY AT CARNAC in southern Brittany includes three separate avenues of menhirs, or standing stones. Seen in this aerial photograph is the Kermario display, consisting of 10 roughly parallel lines of menhirs, hewn from local granite, extending some 4,000 feet.

MOST FAMOUS MONUMENT of the megalithic tradition, Stonehenge is a ring surrounded by a bank and a ditch, situated on the Wiltshire plain of southern Britain. The ring was built in phases, starting in about 2800 B.C., and was completed sometime after 1100 B.C.

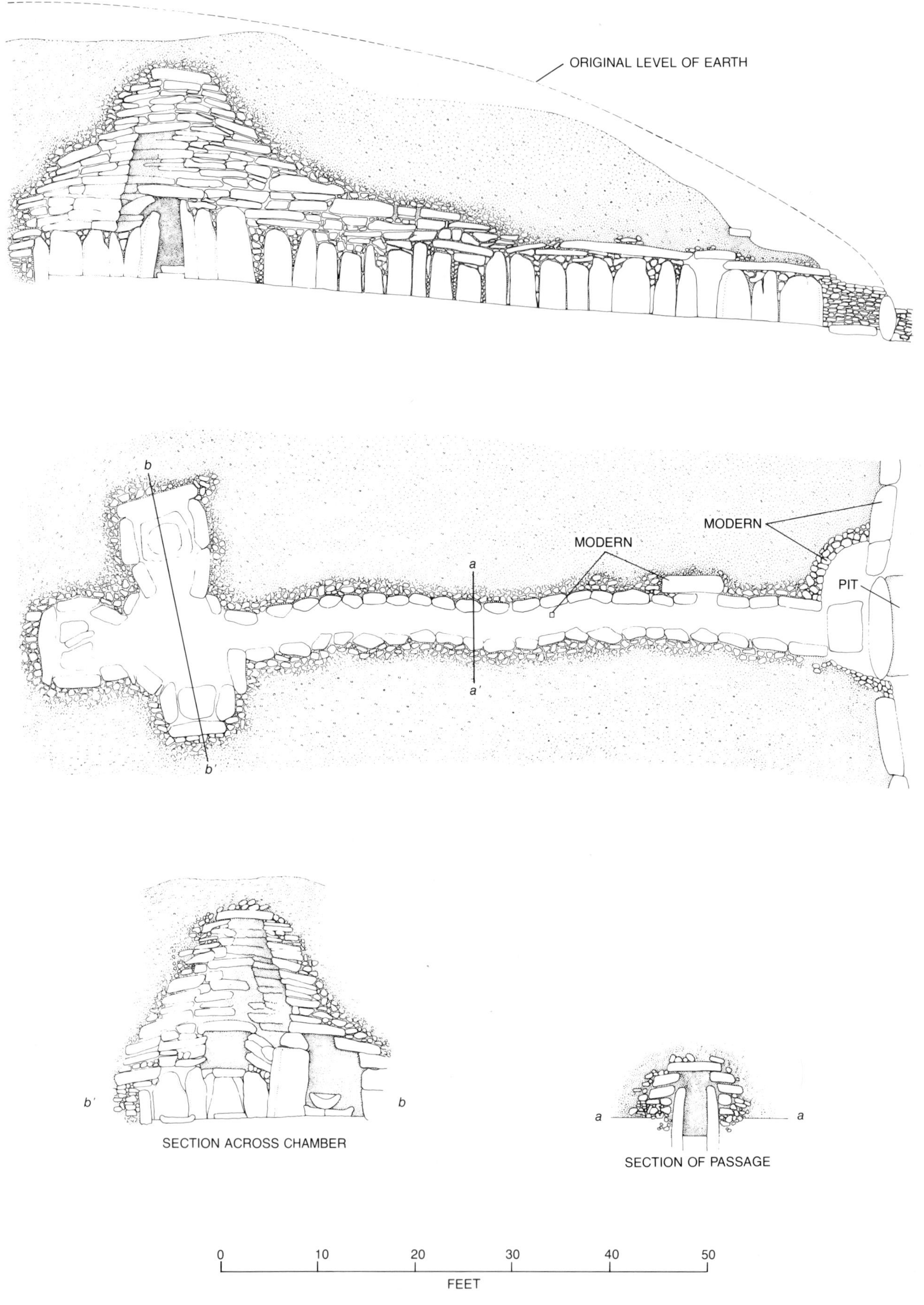

GREATEST BURIAL CHAMBER of the megalithic tradition is Newgrange in County Meath in Eire, shown in elevation at the top and in plan and sections at the bottom. The narrow passage that leads to the burial chamber at the center of the great mound is some 60 feet long; the corbeled vault of the chamber is 20 feet high (*see photograph on opposite page*). Newgrange was built in about 2500 B.C.

man or divine. These are found in southern France and northern Italy, with outlying examples both in Spain and on the Channel Islands. These interesting uprights, the earliest monumental sculpture in the round in human history, can be dated to the end of the third millennium B.C. and the beginning of the second. They are not, however, necessarily connected with the undecorated menhirs.

The second category of megalithic structures is made up of grouped standing stones. The stones are set either in rows, as those at Carnac are, or in what used to be called stone circles. The careful surveys of Alexander Thom, retired professor of engineering at the University of Oxford, have shown that many of the latter monuments are not strictly circular: many are in the form of an ellipse or a flattened ellipse. As a result the term now coming into favor as a description of these megalithic enclosures is stone ring. Some stand alone; some surround a burial mound. Some are associated with rows of stones; some, like the famous monuments of Stonehenge and Avebury in southern Britain and Stenness and Brodgar in Orkney, are surrounded by ditches and banks.

The third category, the burial chamber, constitutes the commonest form of European stone monument. There must be 40,000 to 50,000 of these chambers surviving, and originally there were perhaps twice as many. The largest number of them are found in Spain and Portugal, France, Britain and Ireland, Scandinavia and northern Germany. Some are completely buried under large mounds of earth and stone, some bear traces of partially destroyed mounds and others are entirely freestanding. It was thought in the 19th century that all freestanding chambers were the ruins of chambered mounds, but this is not now thought to be so. Some are the remains of denuded burial mounds but others, such as the portal chambers of Ireland and the great stone galleries of western France, were probably always as they are today.

Many burial chambers exhibit a roofing technique more elaborate than the simple capstone; stones were placed on top of the upright orthostats in such a way as to overlap until they formed a corbeled roof, or vault. Among the most famous surviving corbeled vaults are Maes Howe in Orkney and Newgrange in County Meath in Eire. Maes Howe was broken into by the Vikings, but Newgrange, with its vault rising 20 feet above the ground, has remained intact for 4,500 years. It is one of the wonders of prehistoric Europe.

Many of the stones in these chambers are very large. The capstone of the Mount Browne chamber in County Carlow in Eire is estimated to weigh some 100 tons. The great megalithic chamber at Bagneux, near Saumur in western France, is some 20 meters long by five meters wide, and its roof of four capstones gives three meters of head space to someone standing inside. (It once housed a café!) The capstones are about 60 centimeters thick; the largest of them is estimated to weigh 86 tons.

LOOKING UP to the top of the corbeled vault at Newgrange, this photograph reveals its stepped construction. Each successive layer of slabs was placed closer together until capstones could bridge the narrowed gap. A similar corbeled vault was built at Maes Howe in Orkney.

The fourth category, the megalithic temple, is a limited one. Most of the examples are found in the Mediterranean, on the island of Malta and its neighbor Gozo. The application of the term temple to these great megalithic monuments may conjure up in the minds of some a building comparable in appearance to the pillared structures of dynastic Egypt and Classical Greece. The Maltese monuments are very different. Their solid walls consist of very large slabs of stone, their floor plan includes projecting apses and they were probably roofed with wood beams and thatch. They are certainly among the most impressive prehistoric architectural monuments in the entire Mediterranean area.

That the Maltese structures were temples there is little doubt. They hold no burials and no traces of domestic occupation but do contain many cult objects, including figurines of a female deity and stones decorated with spirals and other designs. There is also no doubt that they date from the fourth millennium B.C. They are thus the earliest example of stone architecture in the Mediterranean and, together with the megalithic chambers of Spain and France, in the entire world.

In medieval times the common folk, and learned men too, thought the great stone monuments must have been the work of giants of long ago. Indeed, the first recorded excavation of a megalithic chamber in Sweden was for the specific purpose of testing this supposition. It was proved wrong; the remains found in the chamber were not those of giants. Later antiquarians sought to explain the megaliths in terms of written history. The structures were variously ascribed to the Romans, the Anglo-Saxons, the Danes, the Goths and the Huns. For example, Herbert, the coiner of the word megalith, argued that because Stonehenge and other British megaliths were not mentioned by Roman historians and visitors to Britain the structures must be post-Roman.

Who and Why

Gradually it came to be accepted that the megaliths were pre-Roman. The pre-Roman inhabitants of northwestern Europe, namely the ancient Gauls and Britons, had been described by Caesar and others as having a class of wise men called Druids. It is not surprising, then, that the megaliths came to be ascribed to the Druids. Some even took the freestanding chambers for Druidic altars.

Over the past two centuries the growth of archaeological excavation has revealed that megalithic chambers were primarily burial places, used collectively by a community or a family over a period of time. Some large chambers have yielded the remains of 200

DOLMEN, OR "TABLE STONE," is the name given to this form of megalithic monument in Brittany. It consists of a single capstone resting on three or more upright supports and is the simplest form of burial chamber. This monument, situated in Pembrokeshire in Wales, is known as the Carreg Samson cromlech, a Welsh word equivalent to dolmen. Some chambers are freestanding; others are mounded over.

LARGER CHAMBER, also in Pembrokeshire, now has only one capstone. This freestanding burial chamber, at Pentre-Ifan, was first recorded by George Owen in his survey of Pembrokeshire published in 1603. Perhaps 50,000 such burial chambers survive in Europe.

individuals or more. Not all megalithic chambers, however, were necessarily tombs. Some, like the freestanding chambers of Ireland and the Loire valley of France, may have been temples, although scarcely Druidic ones. Indeed, the line between a tomb and a temple is not a hard and fast one, as we realize when we look at Christian churches and cathedrals.

The grave goods found in many megalithic chambers are unspectacular: undecorated pots and polished stone axes. In some areas, however, they are rich and remarkable. In Scandinavia heavily decorated pots with oculi, or eye ornaments, are found. In Spain many tombs yield large numbers of schist plaques covered with designs, some of them anthropomorphic. Tombs in Brittany have yielded superbly fashioned polished axes and rings of jade, garnet and other precious materials. These date from the third millennium B.C., long antedating the Chinese and Maya achievements in jade.

EROSION OR VANDALISM had stripped away the mound that once concealed this chambered tomb by the time the artist recorded the monument in the 1840's. Only one capstone still bears some of the former covering of rubble and earth. The engraving on which this sketch of Bryn Celli Ddu in Anglesey in Wales is based appeared in *Archaeologia Cambrensis,* 1847.

The purpose of the menhirs is more difficult to evaluate. Sometimes burials are found at their foot, but they are not tombs. Moreover, such burials cannot even provide a date for the monument, let alone establish its original purpose. Perhaps these single standing stones were intended as territorial markers. Perhaps alternatively they were meant as memorials for the dead, a prehistoric version of the Greek cenotaph, or empty tomb.

The purpose of the menhir alignments and the stone rings is clearly neither funerary nor domestic. Perhaps these monuments were places of assembly where tribes or communities met from time to time for both secular and religious purposes. I see them functioning like the Breton *pardons* of the present day: opportunities for priests to conduct sacred rites, for crops and animals to be blessed, for friends and relatives to meet and enjoy a social occasion, a market and a fair, particularly a hiring fair.

Does such a description fit Stonehenge, the best-known stone ring of them all? First it should be remembered that Stonehenge is a complex monument of several periods and many architectural features, including two circles, two horseshoes and carefully shaped "trilithons" that are a far cry from simple orthostats and capstones. The stones themselves are in part sandstone from the Marlborough Downs and in part "foreign" blue stone from the Preseli hills of Pembrokeshire in southern Wales. There are some 80 of the blue stones, weighing up to four tons each; the distance from Preseli to Stonehenge is 135 miles as the crow flies. The sandstone units, better known as sarsen stones, are also large and were carefully dressed. The largest single component of the sarsen trilithons measures 29 feet eight inches, and the average height of the stones in the sarsen circle is 13 feet six inches. One of the most interesting and architecturally sophisticated devices used by the builders of Stonehenge is what is known in Greek architecture as entasis. This consists of shaping an upright so that the effect of perspective is canceled; when the stones are seen at close range, they do not appear to taper upward but give the optical illusion of being straight-sided.

Measuring the Year

There is no doubt in anyone's mind that Stonehenge was built with its central axis pointing to the midsummer sunrise. Many years ago the British astronomer Sir Norman Lockyer argued that by calculating the exact orientation of Stonehenge he could assign an exact date to the construction of the monument. His conclusion was 1680 B.C. (±200 years). Since then R. J. C. Atkinson of University College, Cardiff, who has done more than anyone by excavation and research to contribute to our modern knowledge of Stonehenge, has pointed out that, owing to errors in Lockyer's original reasoning, his date should be altered slightly. The new reading is 1840 B.C. (±200 years).

The astronomical purpose of Stonehenge and other stone rings was not seriously argued until after World War II, when Gerald S. Hawkins of Boston University proposed in his book *Stonehenge Decoded* (1966) that the monument was a giant calculator for the prediction of eclipses, both lunar and solar. Five years later Thom, in his book *Megalithic Lunar Observatories,* postulated that many megalithic monuments served for observation of the movements and phases of the moon. Thom's surveys had already led him to argue for the existence of a megalithic "yard" measuring 2.72 feet and to suggest that the builders of stone rings had a knowledge of Pythagorean geometry 2,000 years or more before the Greeks. These are extravagant and unconvincing claims; what the builders of megaliths had was a practical knowledge of laying out right-angled triangles.

Many people, no doubt bored by the prosaic account of megaliths to be got from archaeological research, jumped on the Hawkins-Thom bandwagon, accepting the builders of megaliths not only as experts in Pythagorean geometry and possessors of accurate units of mensuration but also as skilled astronomers who studied eclipses, the movements of the moon and the positions of the stars. To me this is a kind of refined academic version of astronaut archaeology. The archaeoastronomy buffs, although they very properly eschew wise men from outer space, very improperly insist on the presence in ancient Europe of wise men with an apparently religious passion for astronomy. It seems to me that the case for interpreting megalithic monuments as astronomical observatories has never been proved. The interpretations appear to be subjective and imposed by the observer. Already new surveys are showing the inaccuracy of some of the earlier observations and undermining the hopes of those who believe the builders of megaliths were slaves of an astronomical cult.

The entire study of megaliths in Europe has been revolutionized not by surveyors with their eye on the moon and the stars but by advances in prehistoric dating. The first of these was the development by Willard F. Libby and his

REVERSING SPIRALS decorate a low wall in a Maltese megalithic temple at Hal Tarxien, near Valetta. The numerous megalithic temples of Malta and nearby Gozo, once believed to have been inspired by Minoan structures, are now known to be indigenous in origin.

SPIRAL DECORATION is predominant among the motifs executed in low relief on this megalithic column at the entrance to New-grange. The decoration, if it is as old as the burial chamber itself, is at least 1,500 years later than the earliest Maltese megalithic temples.

colleagues of carbon-14 dating. The first carbon-14 dates were published 30 years ago, and since then thousands of them have been determined by laboratories all over the world. A more recent geochronological technique, thermoluminescence dating, has confirmed many carbon-14 findings.

The Question of When

Before the carbon-14 revolution—and it has been no less than revolutionary for the field of prehistoric archaeology—the ages of various ancient works of man had either been guessed at or calculated in a regrettably uncertain way by correlations between the dated civilizations of Egypt and Mesopotamia and undated barbarian Europe. Thus in the period between the two world wars it was customary to assign the earliest European megaliths to the Neolithic period, say between 2500 and 2000 B.C., and the great monuments such as Newgrange and Stonehenge to the Bronze Age, between 1800 and 1500 B.C.

Now, thanks to the carbon-14 revolution, we can confidently state how old the megaliths of Europe actually are. The Maltese temples date from 4000 to 2000 B.C. The megalithic chamber tombs of Spain and Portugal date from 3800 to 2000 B.C. The British and Irish tombs date from just after 3800 to 2000 B.C. and the Scandinavian tombs from before 3000 B.C. to, say, 1800 B.C. In the Irish sequence it is good to have a definite date for Newgrange, showing that it was put up in about 2500 B.C. In the British sequence Atkinson has set down the chronological details of Stonehenge: the first phase was from 2800 to 2200 B.C.; the second phase, including the arrival of the blue stones from Wales, was from 2100 to 2000 B.C.; the third phase, which includes three subphases, was from 2000 to 1100 B.C., when the final phase began.

SEMICIRCULAR MOTIF predominates in the low-relief sculpturing of these uprights at the megalithic burial chamber of Gavrinis in France, roughly contemporaneous with Newgrange. Whether the patterns were decorative or whether they had religious meaning is not known.

The dates I have given here, for Stonehenge and for megalithic monuments in general, are what are called calibrated carbon-14 dates. This is to say that they have been adjusted to the corrections based on the study of the rings of the bristlecone pine as displayed in the variation curves plotted by Hans E. Suess of the University of California at San Diego, by R. Malcolm Clark of Monash University in Australia and by others.

How can one explain the origins of these megalithic monuments now that they are accurately dated? There is only one tenable explanation of the menhirs of Brittany and elsewhere in northwestern Europe. They are a local invention; perhaps they represent the translation into stone of an earlier practice of setting up wood posts as cenotaphs or territorial markers or even totem poles.

There is now only one tenable explanation of the Maltese megalithic temples. It used to be argued that they were derived by diffusion from Minoan Crete or from Mycenae or from even farther afield. Carbon-14 chronology now shows them to be earlier than any Minoan, Mycenaean, Egyptian or Sumerian context. The Maltese temples were an indigenous development. Possibly they are aboveground versions of subterranean rock-cut temple tombs. In any event they appear to have no antecedent anywhere, and no structures that can be confidently derived from the Maltese temples have ever been found outside Malta and Gozo.

We now come to the origins of the megalithic chambers and the stone rings. These must not be looked on as isolated phenomena. Instead we must seek to explain them in the context of the Neolithic societies that created them. Elliot Smith's idea that the European megaliths were derived from the mastabas, or stone tombs, of Egypt has no basis in fact and no suggestion of probability. We now know that the megaliths of Europe are older than the mastabas and pyramids of Egypt.

Still another hypothesis, voiced by V. Gordon Childe and others and tenaciously held by most archaeologists during the second quarter of this century, suggested that the megaliths of Europe were built by people who originated in the eastern Mediterranean, particularly in Crete and the islands of the Aegean. Even in the days before carbon-14 dating it was becoming clear that the idea of, for example, deriving great chamber

LARGEST MENHIR in western Europe is this broken specimen at Locmariaquer in Brittany. Three of its four fragments are seen here; the combined length of the four is 22 meters. Whether the menhir ever stood upright is not known; earliest records show it in its present position.

CHRISTIANIZED MENHIR in the Yorkshire village of Rudston, 25 feet high, is the tallest in Britain. The megalithic monument was not thrown down; the graveyard grew up around it.

tombs such as Newgrange and Maes Howe from the domed subterranean tombs of Mycenae was chronologically impossible. As a second line of defense the hypothesis was adjusted backward in time to the vaulted tombs of the Messara in Crete and the rock-cut tombs of the Cyclades. Now both carbon-14 and thermoluminescence determinations show that the European megalithic chambers antedate any of the collective tombs in the eastern Mediterranean.

The New Conclusion

We are therefore forced to conclude that chamber tombs originated independently in at least seven areas of Europe: southern Spain, Portugal, Brittany, northern France, northern Germany, Scandinavia, southern Britain and Scotland. Does this statement appear to be a victory for the "independent evolution" school of archaeological theory over the "diffusionist" school that has held the field for so long?

It is not as simple as that. The Neolithic societies that began to put up megaliths in some areas of Europe in about 4000 B.C. were those that were already building comparable nonlithic or nonmegalithic structures, to wit houses and graves. Many of us think at present that an explanation of the appearance of megalithic chamber tombs in many different parts of Europe must take into consideration three successive phases. The first phase postulates an early European Neolithic tradition of building houses of wood or stone. The second phase involves the transformation of these domestic structures into tombs, still constructed of wood, turf or nonmegalithic stone. The third phase involves the translation of these widespread Neolithic traditions into megalithic architecture in separate areas of Europe that were without doubt interconnected.

The origin of stone rings may be explained in much the same way, although here the phenomenon does not involve seven separate but interconnected areas. The rings are found only in Britain and Ireland. Just as the chamber tomb translates a simpler precursor, so the stone rings cannot be dissociated from the wood-ring monuments now commonly referred to as woodhenges.

I see the origin of stone rings this way. First there were circular clearings in the forests that covered Neolithic Europe in the fifth and fourth millenniums B.C. We can postulate that sacred and secular gatherings took place in these clearings. Next, owing to the agency of man's domestic animals and man himself, the forests disappeared, whereupon artificial clearings were created by setting posts in a ring as a stage for similar gatherings. The third phase was the translation of the wood rings into stone rings. Then finally, as the tour de force of a succession of what one can only call cathedral architects, Stonehenge was built in the middle of the third millennium B.C. and flourished as a temple cum meeting place cum stadium for more than 1,000 years. This brings us back to my earlier question: Does Stonehenge fit the description of megalithic rings in general as sacred and secular meeting places? The answer seems to be emphatically in the affirmative.

Megaliths and Religion

One feels there must have been an impelling faith to inspire the Neolithic people who labored mightily to construct the megaliths of Europe. Tombs, temples, cenotaphs, meeting places—whatever the monuments were—appear to be manifestations of some powerful religious belief including a belief in an afterlife. Was the religion connected with the annual round of the sun, as the orientation of Stonehenge and other stone rings suggests? Was it connected with a mother goddess, as seems to be hinted by the figures from the Maltese temples and those on pottery and on the schist plaques from the tombs in Spain and Portugal? We may never know. Without written sources it is virtually impossible to reconstruct the characteristics, religious and social, of prehistoric societies. We do not know why the hunters of the Upper Paleolithic created paintings, engravings and sculptures in southern France and northern Spain, and we must admit that we also do not know the social and religious ethos of the megalith builders.

Of the thousands of megalithic tombs in Europe a few are decorated with designs carved in low relief or incised on the stone surface. Some in central Germany seem to be representations of tapestry, perhaps the hangings that may have lined the walls of houses. Others, particularly in the Paris basin, are clear representations of a female in frontal view; the eyes, nose and breasts of the deity are emphasized. The majority of the megalithic designs in the tombs of Brittany and Ireland, however, are geometric patterns: spirals, zigzags, lozenges, concentric circles. Perhaps the finest are at Gavrinis in Brittany and at Newgrange. Some, like the spirals on the great stone at the entrance to Newgrange, seem simply decorative. Others are to our eyes a bewildering confusion of what may be signs and symbols. It is important to remember that some of these geometric decorations are buried in the encompassing mounds of chamber tombs and were never meant to be seen; they were deliberately hidden at the time of construction. Why? Are they messages or are they sacred symbols? Whatever their meaning, it is set down in a notation we can never decipher.

In this connection it was discovered only 15 years ago that a representation of a dagger had been engraved on one of the uprights at Stonehenge, as had representations of several axes of Early Bronze Age style. Some fancied the dagger to be a Mycenaean one. This kind of art is quite different from that of the chamber tombs, and of course the representations may have been executed late in the history of Stonehenge. To say that they are Bronze Age graffiti, however, is not to say that Stonehenge was a gigantic Bronze Age lavatory.

The practice of building great stone monuments in Europe died out by 1000 B.C., but the general population need not have simultaneously forgotten the nature and significance of the structures. It is by no means impossible that the folk of the first millennium B.C. continued to congregate and worship at the stone rings, and it is more than possible that the Druidic priesthood of the pre-Roman Celts of Gaul and Britain used them as temples. There is, however, no archaeological evidence of it.

At first Christianity strongly disap-

AVEBURY ENCLOSURE, first recognized as a megalithic circle by John Aubrey in the 17th century, caused him to remark that it "does as much exceed in greatness the so renowned Stoneheng as a Cathedral doeth a parish Church." Few of the 190-odd menhirs that made up the circle and its avenues are visible in this aerial photograph, but the bank and ditch, formed by the quarrying of 200,000 tons of chalk, enclose an area of more than 28 acres. The conical mound visible at upper right, called Silbury Hill, is also manmade.

proved of people who worshiped stones, but gradually there came a new tolerance, which was generous enough for certain menhirs to be Christianized. Indeed, in Spain and Brittany a few megalithic monuments have been incorporated into functioning modern Christian churches. I take this to be a sign that the older faith of the builders survived in some shape or form until at least the Middle Ages of western Europe.

The Builders' Skills

It used to be asked: Who are the megalith builders of ancient Europe and where are their houses and settlements? We now think these questions are the wrong way around. It is the Neolithic villagers of Europe in the fourth and third millenniums B.C. who in certain areas built their tombs and temples in enduring stone. There has been much spoken and written recently about a revolution in our picture of the prehistoric past. Archaeologists are described as having thought of Neolithic peoples as savages, and so the new view of the past that shows them having great mathematical, geometrical and astronomical skills and knowledge dramatically changes our image of prehistoric man.

This thesis makes sense only to those who have never understood the archaeological record and who want to sensationalize prehistory. I have never had any doubt that the Neolithic peoples of Europe were good technicians and skilled engineers. They quarried large stones, transported them for considerable distances and erected them with consummate skill and artistry. We can gain some information about their probable techniques by studying the methods used today in areas such as Assam, where megalithic monuments are still being built. We can measure their accomplishments by noting the difficulties present-day farmers and building contractors encounter in trying to break up the prehistoric structures. For example, late in the past century the capstone of a megalithic chamber near Saumur was moved to be used as a bridge across a local stream. The movers built a number of enormous rollers more than a meter in circumference; each roller was made by lashing the trunks of four oak trees together. Even with the rollers in place 18 pairs of oxen were needed to move the load.

We must never deny the greatness of the megalith builders' achievements. Nor should we deny that from time to time, pausing from their labors at the harvest or at the construction of a monument, they looked as we all do to the sun, the moon and the stars. It is 6,000 years since the first megaliths were built in Malta and Brittany: 4,000 years before the beginning of the Christian Era and 1,000 years before the literate civilizations of Egypt and Mesopotamia. This is a sobering thought when we contemplate, with pride and pleasure, our megalithic patrimony.

III

LINES IN THE PERUVIAN DESERT

The Prehistoric Ground Drawings of Peru

5

by William H. Isbell
October 1978

They look so much as if they were intended to be viewed from the air that they have stimulated much vivid speculation. The archaeological evidence indicates who made them and perhaps also why they were made

In the coastal deserts of Peru are the remains of ancient irrigation systems that held a particular fascination for Paul Kosok of Long Island University, a student of pre-Columbian South America. Some 40 years ago, while he was mapping what he took to be shallow irrigation ditches leading away from tributaries of the Rio Grande on the south coast, Kosok encountered something quite unexpected. In the valley of one such tributary, the Rio Nazca, he came on the giant image of a bird, more than 100 feet long, silhouetted as though it was meant to be viewed from above.

Irrigation ditches seldom if ever form pictures of animals. Kosok inquired among his Peruvian colleagues and learned that many even larger "dirt drawings" of a geometric nature had been noted in the same area. They included long lines (usually called "roads"), zigzags, trapezoids and spirals. Kosok's discovery of a seminaturalistic dirt drawing, however, was a surprise.

Among those who had studied the geometric figures was Toribio Mejía Xesspe of the National University of San Marcos. In a paper published in 1938 he had argued that the ground drawings of the Nazca area were unrelated to irrigation and must have served some ceremonial function in pre-Columbian times. Reconnaissance continued. A huge spider was the next seminaturalistic ground drawing to be added to the list, and others soon followed. Today the total number of such figures exceeds 30.

Before Kosok left Peru in 1941 he speculated that the "roads," at least, might represent ancient astronomical sight lines. He made this suggestion as a possibility worth investigating to Maria Reiche, a German-trained student of mathematics and astronomy who lived in Lima. She has been studying the ground drawings ever since.

What can archaeology and its related disciplines do to explain an odd phenomenon such as the Peruvian ground drawings? Three questions that seem difficult to answer arise immediately: When were the drawings made? Who made them? Why did they make them? In the years since Kosok brought these curiosities to the attention of the general public the first two of the questions have been answered beyond doubt. As for the third question, a number of reasonable conjectures can be proposed. Here I shall review the steps that have led both to the answers and to the conjectures.

The south coast of Peru consists of a range of low hills that runs generally from north to south. Between this coastal rise of land and the foothills of the Andes to the east lies a long lowland basin. For thousands of years the runoff from the higher ground to the west and east carried erosion products into the basin. Most of the eroded material is fine light-colored soil. Occasional flash floods also carried in larger erosion products: stones ranging in size from tiny pebbles to boulders.

Where the Rio Nazca runs down from the foothills to join the Rio Grande these thousands of years of erosional filling have created a wide and level plain. The strong south winds that blew across the plain carried away much of the dusty surface soil, leaving behind a "desert pavement" of pebbles and boulders. In the early morning the stones were damp with dew, but for the rest of the day they were exposed to the hot desert sun. As a result the stones oxidized until their color became a dark red brown.

This change in color actually reduced the amount of wind erosion in the desert. The south wind still blows today, but as the damp stones dry and get hot in the sun their radiation helps to maintain a surface layer of hot air that serves as a buffer against the wind. As for rain erosion, rainfall is so rare along the south coast of Peru that its erosive effects have been negligible for at least 3,000 years.

The geological circumstances that have produced hundreds of square miles of natural blackboard in southern Peru are nowhere seen better than in the plateau above the valley of the entrenched Rio Nazca: an area about 30 miles long and 15 miles wide known as the Pampa Colorada (the Red Plain). Here if one picks up one of the red brown stones, the light soil that lies under it is exposed to view. Pick up a row of rocks and a light-colored line appears. That is how the ground drawings were made: by selective displacement of the desert pavement.

Natural blackboards are well known to archaeologists in areas other than Peru. In southern Britain, where a thin dark soil overlies formations of chalk, the ancient inhabitants selectively exposed the chalk to form, among other images, the great "white horse" effigies of Wiltshire and Kent. Desert pavement was also removed to form figures in the deserts of southern California, as surveys by Dean R. Snow of the State University of New York at Albany have shown. Indeed, if wind and water erosion were as slight in other desert areas of the world as they are on the south coast of Peru, the total number of ground drawings known today might be substantially greater. However that may be, all such figures present a challenge. How can one determine when the work was done?

DESERT "BLACKBOARD" of the ground drawings, the Pampa Colorada near Nazca, appears in the aerial photograph on the opposite page. A variety of drawings are visible. Roadlike lines run in different directions. The broader cleared areas are trapezoidal in outline. A typical spiral appears at the left center. An animal effigy, perhaps a lizard, appears at the bottom right.

The prehistoric pottery found at grave sites in southern Peru, such as the great mortuary center at Cahuachi, is so distinctive in decoration that it has been given the name Nazca, after the modern city and the river valley where many examples of these wares have been unearthed. The Nazca wares were made from about 200 B.C. to about A.D. 600. Students of Andean archaeology call this span in the prehistory of Peru the Early Intermediate Period.

Some Nazca pots are effigies: they are made in the shape of animals and human beings. Others are painted with animal figures: fish, a trophy-bearing killer whale, seabirds, hummingbirds, reptiles, monkeys and llamas. When it was learned that a similar repertory of seminaturalistic animal figures was to be found among the ground drawings of the Pampa Colorada, it was hard to avoid the conclusion that the same prehistoric population was responsible for both creations.

WEST COAST OF SOUTH AMERICA is dominated by the steeply rising Andes. In Peru the foothills of the great mountain range reduce the coastal plain to a narrow strip of desert made fertile only where rivers carry highland rains down to the Pacific. Rain along the coast of southern Peru is almost nonexistent.

This evidence, however, was only iconographic; a more direct kind of evidence was soon forthcoming. A limited amount of broken pottery is to be found on the Pampa Colorada. Since the area is too arid for settlement, it seems reasonable to conclude that the potsherds must have been left by temporary visitors to the desert: casual travelers, traders, pilgrims (if the ground drawings were ritual ones) or work gangs (if the making of the ground drawings was an organized effort). In the early 1970's Gerald S. Hawkins of the Smithsonian Astrophysical Observatory collected a number of sherds from the Pampa Colorada and asked Gordon R. Willey of Harvard University and John H. Rowe of the University of California at Berkeley to identify them. Willey and Rowe found that 85 percent of the sherds were Nazca wares. The remaining 15 percent were wares of a subsequent period: the interval between A.D. 900 and 1400. At about the same time Rodger Ravines of the National Cultural Institute of Peru made a collection of sherds from sites on the periphery of the Pampa Colorada; they proved to be exclusively Nazca wares. The peripheral sites give the appearance of being temporary shelters; perhaps they were camps for work gangs.

This evidence, a positive identification of users of Nazca pottery as visitors to the ground drawings, taken together with the presence of the same animal figures in both mediums, settled once and for all the question of who had so artfully disturbed the desert pavement of the Pampa Colorada. The fact remains that the interval between 200 B.C. and A.D. 600 is almost a millennium. Might it be possible to find more precisely when during the Early Intermediate Period such activity took place? Precise dating of this kind became possible after World War II with the development of carbon-14 analysis. Some of the long lines laid out on the Pampa Colorada terminate where a wood stake was driven into the ground. In 1953 W. Duncan Strong of Columbia University collected a sample from such a stake for carbon-14 analysis. The analysis showed that the wood was from a tree that had been cut down in A.D. 525 (±80), very late in the Early Intermediate Period. To be sure, the finding can at best only suggest when the long line associated with this particular stake was laid out (and perhaps not even that if one considers that the stake might be the second, the third or the 30th replacement of the original one). Nevertheless, the carbon-14 date falls within the limits of Nazca times and therefore lends weight to the other evidence.

Now that the questions "Who?" and "When?" are answered, it is time to consider the question "Why?" Again archaeology and its related disciplines, ethnology in particular, offer useful clues. For example, it may seem peculiar that any population would invest a significant amount of energy in constructing displays that are best seen from the air rather than from the ground. Indeed, the people who made the chalk figures in Britain did so on hillsides where they are clearly visible. On the other hand, parallels to the Nazca displays do exist. Among the ambitious earthworks raised by the Hopewell cultists of pre-Columbian North America are a number of figures that would certainly be less readily recognized from the ground than from the air. The great serpent mound in Ohio is an outstanding example. The same is true of the California desert figures documented by Snow. Since this feature of the Nazca ground drawings is not unique, it would seem unnecessary to suppose the drawings were made to be viewed from the air, even if one could imagine how it was done.

What about the cost in energy that had to be paid to shift stones and create a ground drawing? Here again archaeology offers a clue. Elsewhere in Peru during the Early Intermediate Period the local farming populations were engaged in work-gang labor of staggering proportions. For example, the largest prehistoric pyramid in Peru is located in the valley of the Rio Moche. An enormous temple platform, the Huaca del Sol, called for the manufacture of 140 million adobe bricks. Studies of the construction methods and of the bricks themselves indicate that the work was done by crews of unskilled laborers. Each crew, probably composed of men recruited from a single region, manufactured its own bricks, transported them to the construction site and there built one or more of the columns of brick that make up the pyramid. Each crew's work is still identifiable by the distinctive marks on different batches of brick.

The pyramidal structures and other monumental buildings of the Early Intermediate Period in northern and central Peru evidently represent the apogee of a pre-Columbian period of Andean ceremonial architecture. Some temple platforms are also found along the south coast of Peru, but they are modest compared with the massive adobe edifices raised to the north. By the same token ground drawings were laid out at desert sites along the north and central coast of Peru, but they are modest by Nazca standards.

Those who are not familiar with the ground drawings may find it hard to compare the effort involved in their creation with the effort involved in making and laying bricks. The reason is that the discussion so far has been confined largely to the animal effigies. In terms of the tonnage of stone shifted the animal portrayals represent only a fraction of the total energy input. For example, an animal may be sketched out by a single continuous line. Many of the lines, however, originate at a distant trapezoid or rectangle and then return to it.

The geometric figure that provides the point of origin may be more than a kilometer long. The same figure may also be the point of origin for a series of zigzags or for a single line that runs straight across the desert eight kilometers or more before terminating at a stake or a heap of stones. Only if one were to measure the effort required to duplicate a representative ground drawing today would it be possible to estimate the total prehistoric investment of labor at the Pampa Colorada in any but the most general way. It nonetheless seems reasonable to suppose the ground-drawing efforts in the Nazca area represent an energy investment roughly comparable to that which created the monumental adobe structures to the north.

Whether or not the two efforts were equal in scale, both seem to have fulfilled similar economic functions. These functions are related to the drafting of community labor for public works. The nationwide controls exercised by the Incas at the time of Pizarro's conquest of Peru are well known. It is less well known that the earliest of the Incas' imperial predecessors had a similarly centralized regime. Whereas the Incas' capital was at Cuzco, that of the earlier empire was at Huari.

Provincial administrative centers, all linked to Huari, collected and stored large quantities of foodstuff and goods produced in the rural hinterland. If there were local or regional variations in agricultural or cottage-industry productivity, the overall economy was balanced by adding to the centralized stores or by exchanges among the provincial centers. Such economic uniformity enabled the population of prehistoric Peru to expand and then to stabilize at a level higher than that in the preceding period of regional autonomy.

Such was far from the case during the Early Intermediate Period. That some kind of control was exercised over community labor is apparent in the construction of the great adobe temple platforms. There is no evidence, however, that the people of the period built administrative structures or storage facilities such as were characteristic of the imperial regimes of Huari and Cuzco. This suggests that each region was subject to local economic fluctuations and directly related population changes.

Consider the effect of such fluctuations. A series of good agricultural years in a region would have led, in the absence of any local control mechanism, to a population increase. Thereafter a series of bad years would have been disastrous for the larger population. The way to avoid this kind of response to economic fluctuations is to keep the

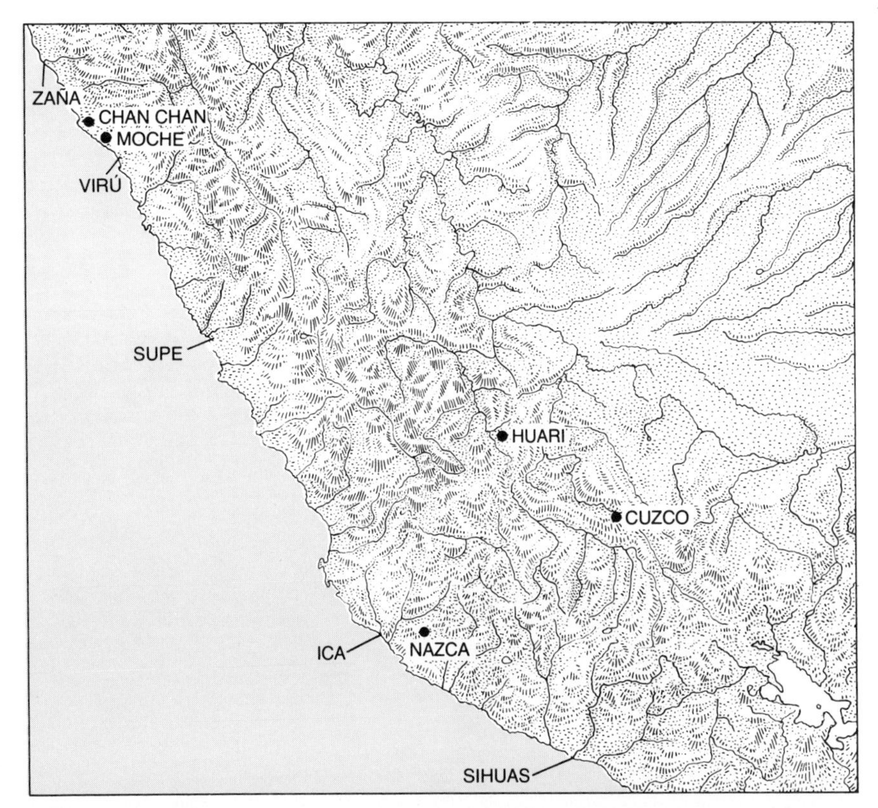

GROUND DRAWINGS have been located in the coastal deserts of Peru from as far north as the Virú valley to as far south as the Sihuas valley. They are found in the vicinity of Supe, Lima and Ica and have been reported but not confirmed in the Zaña valley. They are commonest in the vicinity of Nazca, where ancient graves have been found to contain distinctive pottery.

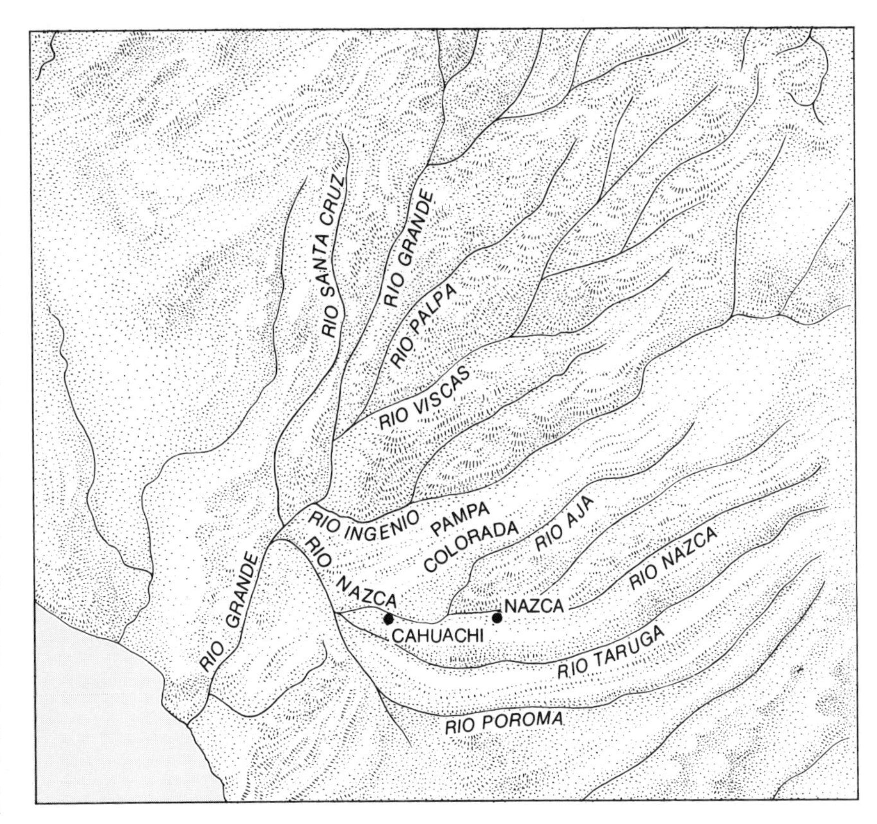

DESERT PLATEAU north of the Rio Nazca, the Pampa Colorada, is 30 miles long and 15 miles wide. It has the greatest concentration of ground drawings in Peru. The nearby ruins of Cahuachi, a mortuary site of the Peruvian Early Intermediate Period (200 B.C.–A.D. 600), is one of the numerous sources of the Nazca-style pottery that is indigenous to this part of Peru.

KILLER WHALE is the subject of this ground drawing on the Pampa Colorada (*top*). The circular object seen to dangle below the jaw of the whale is a human head, a war trophy that is regularly depicted in Peruvian pottery designs and other decorations of the pre-Columbian period. The effigy pot (*bottom*) also depicts a killer whale, complete with a trophy head. The effigy was unearthed near the Pampa Colorada; it was made during the Early Intermediate Period of Peruvian prehistory. It appears here courtesy of Wilfredo Loayza.

surplus of the good years from fueling an increase in population. An artificial leveling of the economy will inhibit population growth, holding the total below the one that taxes the maximum carrying capacity of the regional economy.

How might this leveling be achieved? One way is to cultivate a common concern with ceremonial activities that call for a large investment of labor. In Nazca times the kinds of centralized food storage characteristic of the Huari and Cuzco regimes would not have existed, and surpluses would have been dispersed not on a provincial and state level but on a local or even familial one. If an autonomous region suffered bad years, drawing on such decentralized stores would help to tide it over. If, on the other hand, the region enjoyed good years, the accumulated private stores could be tapped to provide support for local work gangs engaged in ceremonial activities such as building temple platforms or laying out ground drawings. In either event the population would remain relatively stable.

Seen in this light the basic function (or, if one prefers the terminology of Darwinian evolution, the selective advantage) of laying out ground drawings has nothing to do with whether they were viewed from the ground or from above, or for that matter with whether they were viewed at all. The function lies in the fact that societies with a cultural mechanism for investing unpredictable surpluses in ceremonial activities have a selective advantage over societies lacking such a mechanism. They regulate their population, and societies that do not are doomed to cycles of "boom" and "bust."

Were the leaders of these regional societies in the Early Intermediate Period of Peruvian prehistory consciously aware of such complex concepts as the allocation of surplus resources to prevent an excess of population? Whether or not they were aware of them makes little difference; those who had such a system eventually replaced their neighbors, and the successful ceremonial behavior was thereby perpetuated. At the conscious level such continuity may have been based on a decision-making process no more profound than the argument that "this is the way we have always done it."

Much human behavior is based on this kind of "custom," a simple following of behavior patterns that have been successful in the past. In nonliterate societies the information on such behavior is often codified as ritual to ensure that it is conveyed to future generations. A pertinent example is contained in the study of a modern but barely literate Peruvian highland village by my wife, Billie Jean Isbell of Cornell University.

Her research has revealed that these farming families depend for their economic independence on a strategy of cultivating a variety of crops at different elevations. The villagers have a specific name for each crop zone. The distinction between the zones has been symbolized by the construction of a chapel at the boundary of each one. The annual harvest ritual involves a series of visits to the chapels and the harvesting of a sample of the produce grown in each zone. A cross is taken from each chapel and is decorated with the harvested plants. All the crosses are then brought to the village and presented to the village priest.

Even if a young villager fails to learn how to farm from his family and his village elders, the message of this annual ritual could scarcely be overlooked:

PERUVIAN SCHOLAR Maria Reiche (*left*) demonstrates the surveying methods she has used for more than 30 years in recording Nazca ground drawings. Her audience is Patricia J. Knobloch of the State University of New York at Binghamton, a visiting archaeologist. The rocks that form the "desert pavement" at the Pampa Colorada range in size from pebbles to boulders.

ZIGZAG PATTERN on the Pampa Colorada was formed, as were all the ground figures, by selectively removing the rocks that cover the desert floor, thereby revealing the lighter-colored earth under them. Here some of the shifted rocks were piled up at the bends of the figure.

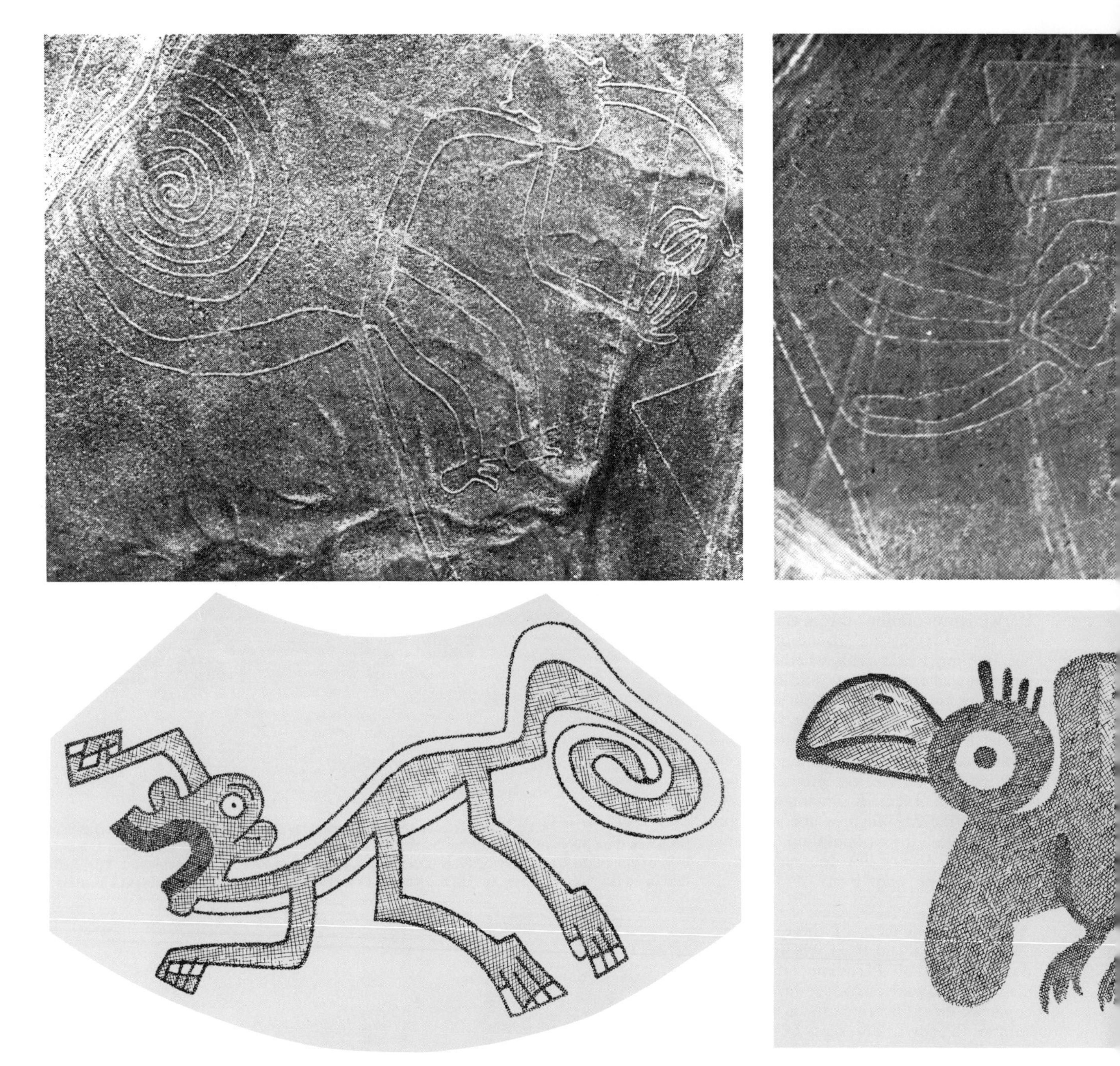

THREE GROUND FIGURES (*top*) are compared with portrayals of the same animals that appear on Nazca pottery (*bottom*). At left is a stylized monkey with a much exaggerated tail. The drawing of a monkey appears on a double-spout pot photographed by Loayza. The bird figure at center may represent a frigate bird; these birds have a conspicuous throat pouch. The drawing of a similar bird figure ap-

"Here are the sections that divide the earth. Here are the crops that are grown in each section. It pleases God (and the priest) that all these crops are grown every year." Conscious recognition of the economic advantages of mixed farming may not even exist among the villagers, but the pattern of behavior that the ritual symbolically reinforces helps to protect its practitioners from the danger of single-crop failure and the social disruption that accompanies dependence on wage labor.

R. Tom Zuidema of the University of Illinois has reconstructed similar rituals observed by the people of Cuzco when the city was the capital of the Inca empire. At that time imaginary lines radiated in all directions from Cuzco. The lines were imaginary in that they were unmarked, but the orientation of each line was indicated by a series of shrines. Every day of the year a different kin group among the city dwellers worshiped at a different shrine; in effect the floor of the valley of Cuzco had been mapped out in an annual ritual calendar. Information about the agricultural cycle, social obligations, military activities and many other topics was thereby symbolically communicated to the people of Cuzco. The fact that the Incas felt a concern for this kind of informative mapping is demonstrated by the ground plan of the capital itself. The Incas called Cuzco "the puma" and its inhabitants "members of the body of the puma." The city was laid out in the shape of a puma, although the animal form was somewhat distorted by the fact that it had to conform to the topography of the valley.

I have suggested that the ground drawings at Nazca were primarily a product of social mechanisms for regulating the balance between resources and population. Zuidema's findings on the

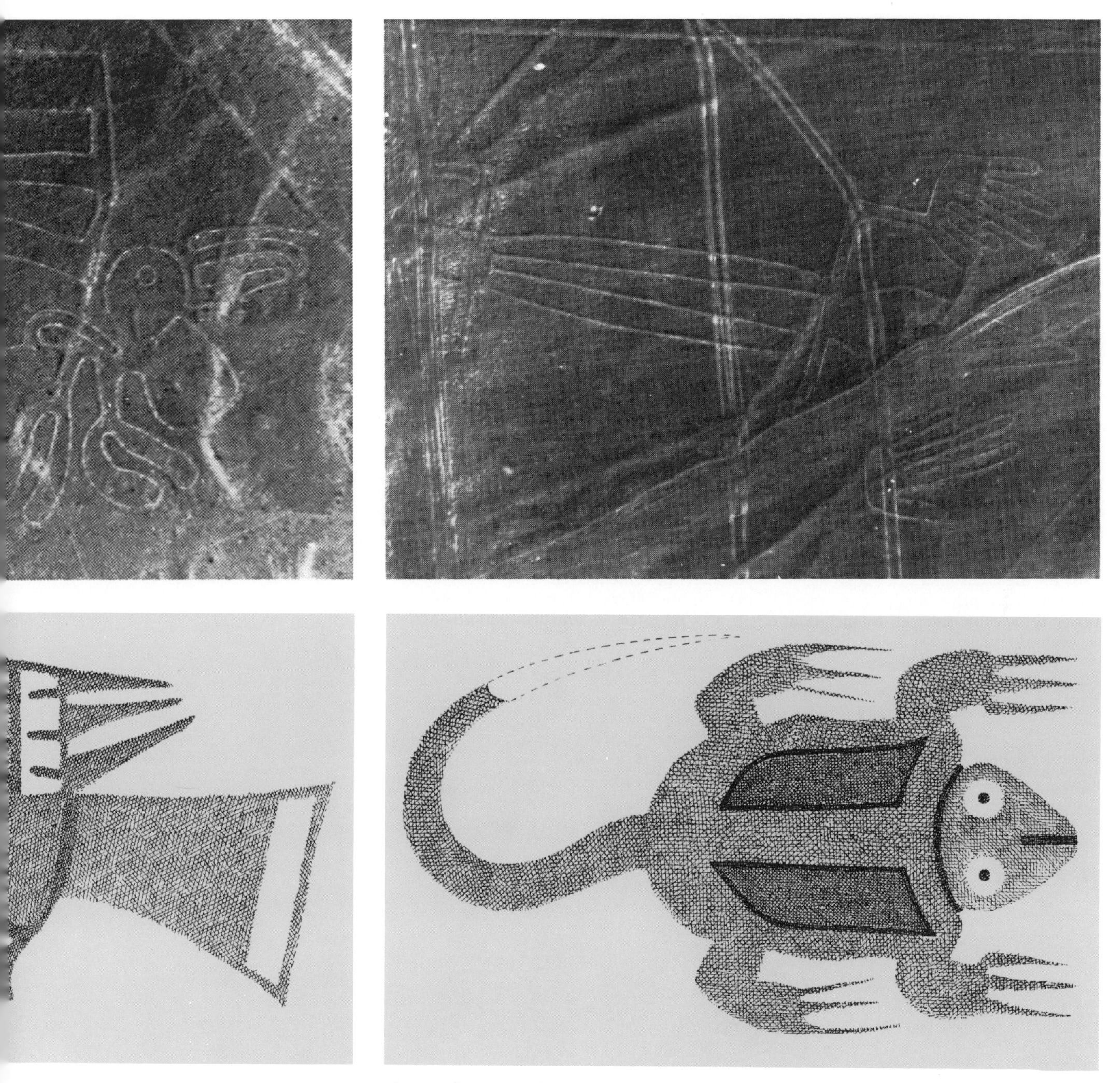

pears on a Nazca pot in the collection of the Putnam Museum in Davenport, Iowa. The lizardlike figure at the right has a long tail that does not appear in this aerial photograph, but its hind legs were not executed with the same detail as its forelegs. The drawing of a similar lizard appears on a Nazca pot in the collection of the Robert H. Lowie Museum of Anthropology at University of California at Berkeley.

symbolic ground-mapping practices of the Incas (who eventually succeeded to authority over the Nazca region) and Billie Jean Isbell's documentation of agricultural ritual among the highland Indians of Peru today suggest that the Nazca ground drawings also contained certain symbolic information, mapped on the ground for successive generations to observe, recognize and memorize.

What were these mapped messages? As Reiche has pointed out for many years, certain of the Pampa Colorada lines mark the position of the sun at the summer and winter solstices and certain other lines also appear to have calendrical significance. A computerized analysis of line orientation conducted by Hawkins, although it failed to demonstrate that a majority of the lines have astronomical significance, showed that twice as many of them were oriented with respect to annual solar and lunar extremes than would be expected on the basis of chance.

Both studies indicate that at least some of the Nazca ground drawings have calendrical potential. The mapping of calendrical data on the ground, if it was combined with ritual observations, could have communicated not only information of agricultural significance but also other kinds of information useful to a complex but preliterate society faced with a pressing need to store the knowledge acquired from generations of experience.

To return to the questions I raised at the outset: Can archaeology and related disciplines determine when the ground drawings of the Pampa Colorada were made, who made them and why? It seems clear that the answers to the first two questions are that most if not all of the drawings are the work of the same people who shaped and painted the lovely pottery of Nazca in the period between 200 B.C. and A.D. 600. The graves of this prehistoric farming people and the ruined towns and villages where they once lived both lie near the drawings.

As for the question why, it also seems clear that the making of the drawings, like the building of the enormous adobe-brick structures to the north, served to regulate population increases related to changes in the available energy. It is one thing, of course, to recognize the function served by energy investments of this regulatory kind and quite another to gain an understanding of the tangible form the investment takes. I nonetheless find it a credible hypothesis that the ground drawings reflect the general need by the various preliterate societies of Peru to record or, perhaps more accurately, to store significant information about how their system worked.

The storage of inventories by means of the well-known Peruvian string-and-knot system of enumeration, the quipu, was evidently a practice adopted early in the prehistory of the Andes. Calendrical data, particularly when their use calls for the cross-check of actual astronomical observation, might be impractical or impossible to store by means of quipus. I suggest that such kinds of information were symbolically coded and recorded in the most durable medium available: the surface of the earth itself.

If the Pampa Colorada ground drawings were the only ones in Peru, such a hypothesis might carry little weight. Actually ground drawings have been found in many other places. A rectangular figure 60 meters long and 30 meters wide and including geometric "decorations" has been mapped in an area above the Sihuas valley south of Nazca. "Road" lines are present in the Ica valley just north of Nazca, in the vicinity of Lima still farther to the north, north of Lima in the Virú valley near the monumental Huaca del Sol and reportedly in the Zaña valley 180 kilometers north of Virú. In the Supe valley between Lima and Virú, Alberto Carbajal, Carlos Williams and I recently photographed previously unreported lines, geometric figures, chains of spirals and a ground drawing of a human face 43 meters wide. Low-altitude aerial photography and ground surveys of other Peruvian desert-pavement areas might reveal many more figures. It is plain that energy was invested in the production of ground drawings even in parts of Peru where the major community-labor investment was in the construction of adobe platforms and other monumental works. The ground drawings along the north and central coast may be modest by Nazca standards, but they demonstrate that such figures were not exclusively a south-coast phenomenon.

In the centuries following the Early Intermediate Period the energy investment in temple platforms continued but on a far smaller and less impressive scale. The same appears to be true of the ground figures. Evidently the emerging state authority centered at Huari saw to it that the main community effort was redirected into the construction of administrative buildings, storage facilities, fortifications and what seem to have been manufacturing centers. Regional autonomy gave way to centralized authority, setting the stage for the eventual rise of the Inca empire. One can logically expect that the earlier practice of regional data storage and retrieval, written on the earth and vested in local ritual, then slowly ceased to be.

IV

PYRAMIDS

6 The Tombs of the First Pharaohs

by Walter B. Emery
July 1957

Before the kings of Egypt made pyramids, they were buried in great brick-lined pits topped by rectangular buildings. These structures provide clues as to how civilization came to the Valley of the Nile

When the famous British archaeologist Flinders Petrie published his *History of Egypt* in 1894, he devoted only 10 pages of it to the period before 2680 B.C. Yet by that time there had already been three dynasties of Egyptian kings. Egyptologists had learned much about the succeeding 27 dynasties by archaeological excavation, but their knowledge of the first pharaohs was based only on the lists of kings compiled by later Egyptians and on the writings of Greek and Roman historians. Indeed, some authorities believed that these kings were figures of myth and legend rather than men who really lived. But at the turn of the century the pick of the excavator revealed many monuments of the First Dynasty, and the shadowy figures of the first pharaohs stepped forth onto the stage of history to tell their story of the rise of civilization in the valley of the Nile.

The most important of these discoveries was made in 1895 at Abydos, a site on the Nile 300 miles south of Cairo. Here the French Egyptologist Emile-Clément Amélineau discovered a group of graves consisting of great pits lined with brick. In 1899 Petrie began to work at Abydos, and in two years of brilliant research he established its tombs as monuments of the kings of the First and Second Dynasties. He was also able to identify the royal owner of each tomb and to establish the order of his succession. Originally each brick-lined pit was roofed with timber and surmounted with a superstructure. In all cases this part of the building has disappeared, and no indication of its precise form exists. We do know, however, that because the tombs are so close to one another the superstructures cannot have covered an area much larger than the pits themselves. Each tomb was surrounded by numerous graves which contained the bodies of slaves sacrificed to continue their service to the king in the afterworld.

Petrie believed that the kings of the First Dynasty were actually buried at Abydos, and until recently there was no reason to doubt this conclusion. Later excavations strongly suggest, however, that the kings were buried not at Abydos but at Sakkara, far down the Nile [*see map on page 80*]. Sakkara, the vast cemetery of ancient Memphis, is best known as the site of a great stepped pyramid of the Third Dynasty. At its north end are the remains of tombs which had long been recognized as perhaps even older than this pyramid. But it was not until 1912 that any really serious research was undertaken at North Sakkara. The late J. E. Quibell, then Chief Inspector of the Egyptian Department of Antiquities, excavated for two seasons and proved the existence of First Dynasty tombs far better preserved than those at Abydos.

The site was still not considered especially promising because it had been systematically ravaged by tomb-robbers for more than 5,000 years, and so after the interruption of Quibell's work by World War I the site lay untouched until 1930. Then his successor, the late C. M. Firth, resumed the excavations. Firth cleared several more First Dynasty tombs, the most notable of which was known as 3035. The paneled exterior and burial pit of this great structure were excavated, but its interior was left untouched. This was because it was believed that the interior of the superstructures of such monuments was a solid network of brick walls filled with rubble. The excavation of Tomb 3035 was not very productive, for the burial chamber had been plundered and replundered in ancient times. Nonetheless Firth was able to establish that the tomb had been built during the reign of Udimu, fifth king of the First Dynasty. Firth

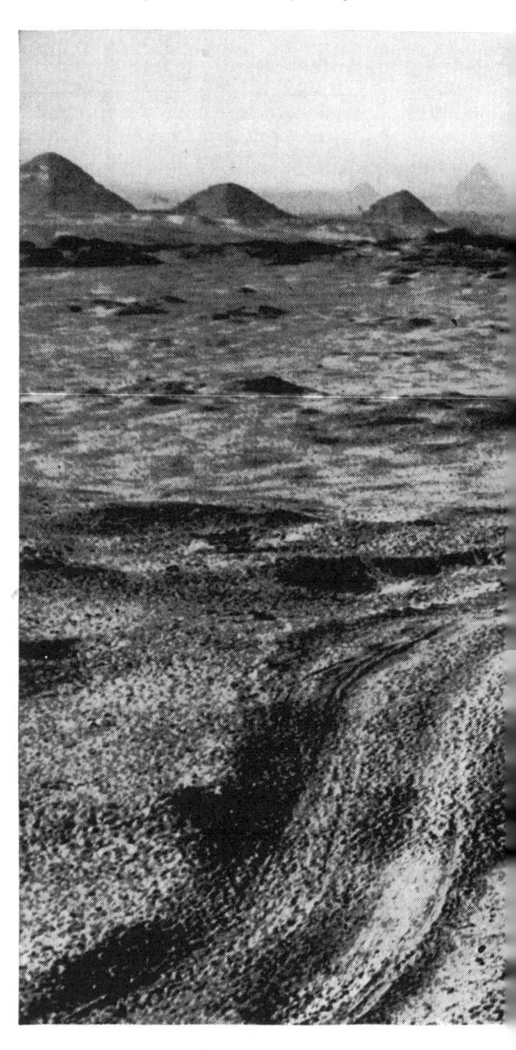

EXCAVATED TOMBS of the pharaohs of the First Dynasty are on the right side of

died suddenly in 1932, and once again the exploration of North Sakkara was interrupted.

In 1935, when the Director General of the Department of Antiquities instructed me to reclear the tombs, I also turned my attention to Tomb 3035. In order to determine certain details of its construction I cut rather ruthlessly into the big brick superstructure and found that it was not just a solid mass of brickwork and rubble but was divided up into a series of 45 storerooms, many of which had escaped the attention of the ancient tomb-robbers. In these storerooms we found a great collection of funerary equipment—food, tools, weapons, games and drinking vessels—lying where they had been placed 5,000 years before. Inscriptions on the clay seals of jars led us to believe that the tomb belonged to a great noble named Hemaka, vizier of the pharaoh Udimu. This was the greatest single discovery of First Dynasty material that had been made up to that time. Its importance was at once appreciated by the Egyptian Government and I was given permission to explore the whole area systematically.

Digging continued from 1935 until the beginning of World War II; one great tomb after another was cleared, each showing that civilization during the period of the First Dynasty was far more advanced than we had supposed. Tombs contemporaneous with the kings Hor-Aha, Zer, Udimu, Enezib and Ka-a were discovered—all much larger and more elaborate in design than their counterparts at Abydos. We knew that these kings originated at This near Abydos, but that they conquered the lower Nile Valley and established their capital at Memphis. Thus it seemed possible and even probable that the tombs at Sakkara were their actual burial places, and that the structures at Abydos were empty monuments. Only further excavation could confirm this theory, but at the outbreak of the war the work was shut down. With the exception of a short season in 1946, nothing further was done at North Sakkara until 1952. In that year an arrangement was made whereby the Egypt Exploration Society reopened the excavations on behalf of the Department of Antiquities. The clearance is still in progress.

In 1952 we discovered a tomb which probably belonged to Uadji, the third pharaoh of the First Dynasty; in the following year we excavated another which we ascribed to Ka-a, the last king of the dynasty. A third large tomb was cleared in 1955, and although its ownership could not be established it supplies conclusive evidence that all the burials almost certainly belonged to the kings, queens and princes of the First Dynasty.

These big tombs of the First Dynasty have the same fundamental design: a large pit cut in the ground, within which were built the burial chamber and subsidiary rooms [*see drawings on pages 82 and 83*]. Here were stored the owner's most precious possessions. This

this photograph of the area around North Sakkara, 15 miles from Cairo. In the distance at the far left are three pyramids of the Fifth Dynasty. Beyond them are the three famous pyramids built by the Fourth Dynasty kings Khufu (Cheops), Khafra and Menkaura.

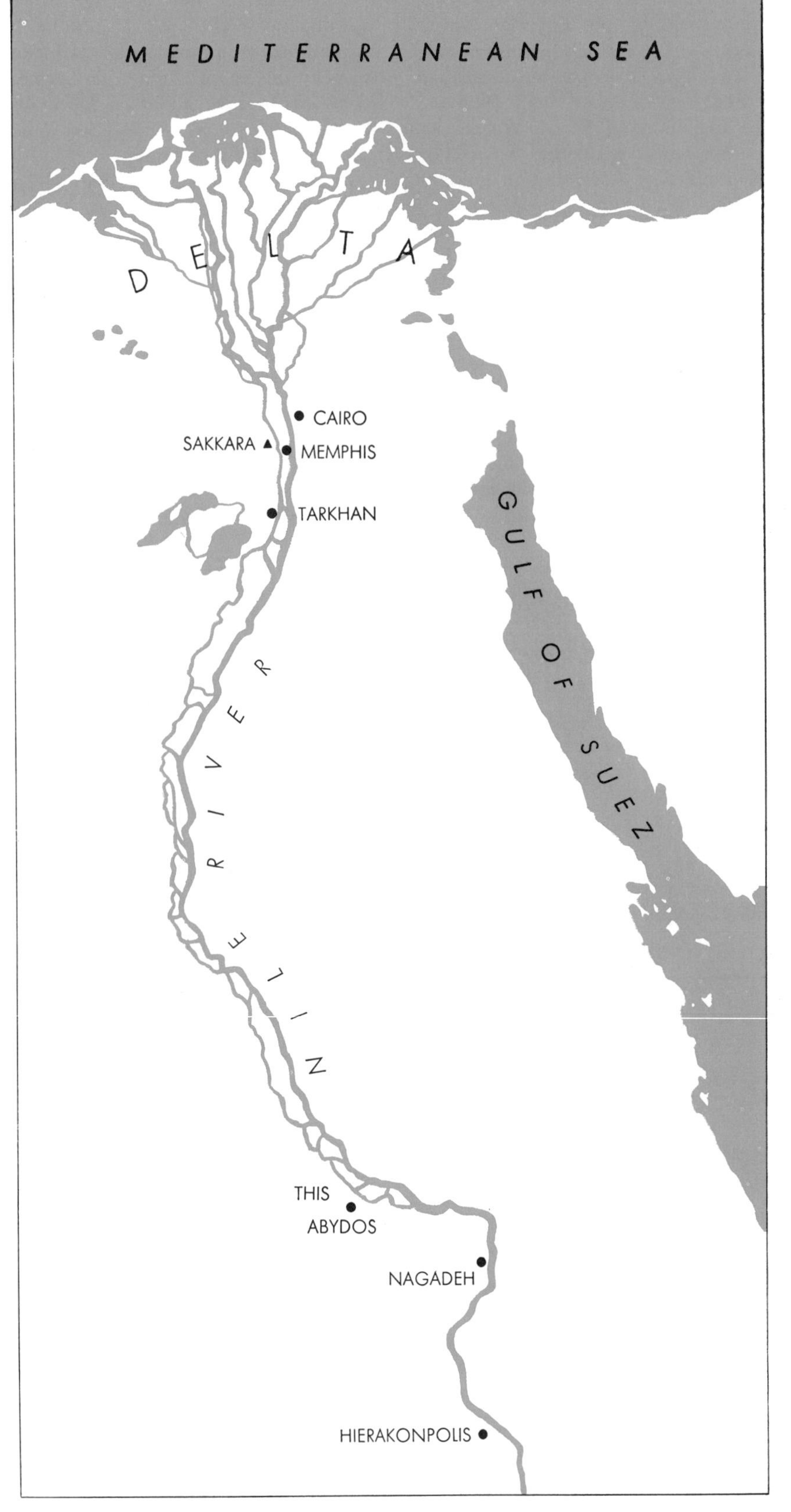

SITES mentioned in this article are located on a map of the Nile Valley. The pharaohs of the First Dynasty originated at This but later established their capital at Memphis. It was once thought that they were buried at Abydos, but it now appears that their graves are at Sakkara. Tarkhan, Nagadeh and Hierakonpolis are other sites of the First Dynasty.

substructure was covered by a large rectangular superstructure of brick, enclosing chambers in which were stored reserve supplies for the use of the deceased in afterlife. This was only the general scheme of the funerary edifice; refinements and developments occurred in rapid succession throughout the 250-odd years of the dynasty. The developments were confined principally to the substructure; the superstructure increased in size but remained largely unchanged. These great buildings, made only of unbaked brick, were undoubtedly dummy copies of the actual palaces of the kings. Although they now stand only five feet above their foundations, there is evidence that they originally rose to a height of not less than 30 feet. The elaborate recess-paneling of their exteriors was gaily painted with geometrical designs simulating the colored matting which adorned the interior walls of buildings at that time.

Although the burial chambers were ravaged and, in many cases, set afire by plunderers, we can reconstruct them with considerable certainty. The deceased lay slightly bent on his right side within a great wooden sarcophagus measuring about 10 by six feet. Outside the sarcophagus were furniture, games for the amusement of the deceased, and his last meal, served in vessels of alabaster, diorite, schist and pottery. These meals were of an elaborate character, consisting of soup, ribs of beef, pigeon, quail, fish, fruit, bread and cake. We found such a meal remarkably preserved in a tomb of the early Second Dynasty, and from fragments found with burials of the First Dynasty we have every reason to suppose that the same rich repast was left during the earlier period. Other rooms in the substructure were devoted to the storage of wine and food, furniture, clothing, games, tools and weapons of flint and copper. Similar objects were stored in the chambers of the superstructure: hundreds of great wine jars, furniture inlaid with ivory, toilet implements, agricultural equipment—all the appurtenances of a well-organized and highly developed civilization.

The principal evolution in the design of the substructure was the introduction of a stairway entrance which enabled the architect to build the whole funerary edifice before the burial. Before this innovation had been introduced the superstructure was built after the burial—obviously an unsatisfactory arrangement. At the end of the First Dynasty a small funerary temple was built at the north side of the tomb; both tomb and temple

SUPERSTRUCTURE of a First Dynasty tomb is exposed by excavation. The recessed walls of the superstructure originally stood at least 30 feet high and were painted with geometrical designs. This is probably the tomb of Queen Meryt-Nit of the First Dynasty.

CLAY MODEL of an ancient Egyptian estate is excavated beside the tomb of Hor-Aha, the first king of the First Dynasty. Such models may have been small-scale copies of the royal estates, presumably to be re-created for the use of their owners in the afterlife.

were enclosed by walls with an entrance to the east. In this final evolution of the First Dynasty tomb we have the prototype of the pyramid complex of later dynasties.

We still have much to learn about the earliest First Dynasty tombs, which are perhaps the oldest examples of monumental architecture in the world. They are not entirely what they seem. In the course of our excavations we have often been puzzled to discover stairways and passages which lead nowhere. For a time we were inclined to dismiss these mysterious features as the result of alterations in the architect's plans. Now we know that the tombs were built in two distinct stages. First they were raised to serve some unknown purpose; then, after this purpose was fulfilled, they were altered so that they could serve

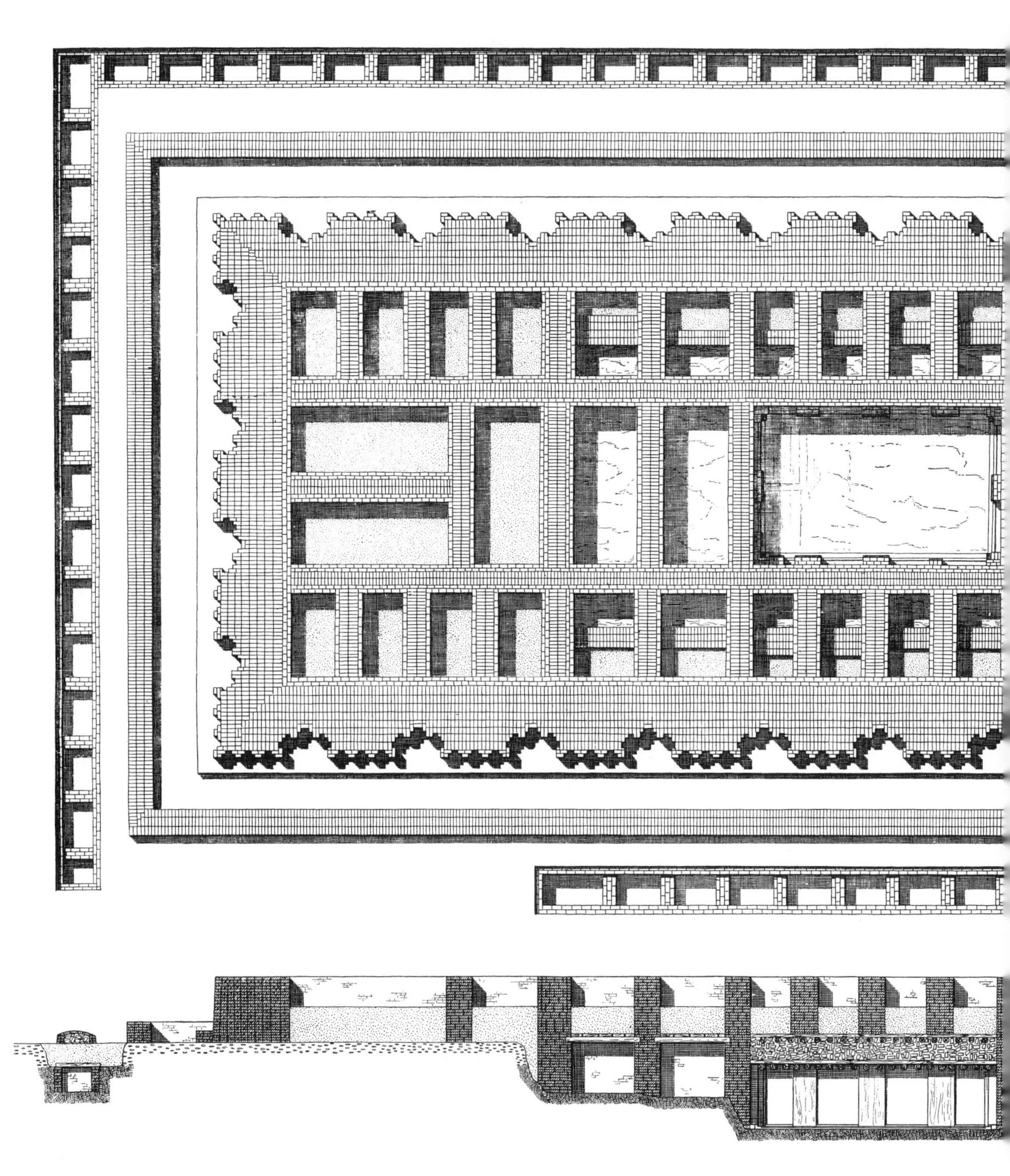

TOMB IS RECONSTRUCTED in plan and elevation by these drawings. This is Tomb 3504 at Sakkara. It is dated to the reign of Uadji, third king of the First Dynasty. The tomb is roughly 200 feet long and 100 feet wide. In the center is the burial chamber. Around

their final function as a house of the dead. We are still entirely ignorant as to the purpose of the original structure, and we can only hope that further excavation will give us the answer to this fascinating question.

The complete funerary installation consisted not only of the tomb, but also of surrounding graves of retainers sacrificed to accompany the king in death as in life. These small graves are of great interest, for we often find objects buried with the dead retainer which indicate his occupation: paint pots with the artist, model ships with the shipmaster, varieties of pottery with the potter, and so on. Around the tombs we frequently find the remains of gardens with rows of trees and plants. Near one tomb is a clay model of an estate with houses, granaries and fields. It is tempting to see in this model an exact copy of the royal estate, to be re-created in the next world for the service of its dead owner. Beside the tomb of Udimu are the remains of a wooden ship to carry the pharaoh with the celestial gods in their voyage across the heavens. This vessel, which was 50 feet long, was built 400 years before the recently discovered ship of Cheops.

There are still other sites of the First Dynasty awaiting excavation. It is thus a little early to come to any conclusion regarding the origin of civilization in the Nile Valley. Enough has been disclosed, however, to show that a highly developed culture existed in Egypt by 3000 B.C. In assessing this culture we must remember that we do so on evidence which has survived 5,000 years of destruction by nature and man. But even in their ruined state the magnificent monuments of Sakkara, Abydos and other sites show that they were built by a people with an advanced knowledge of architecture and a mastery of construction in both brick and stone. The scattered contents of their tombs show that they had a well-developed written language, a knowledge of the preparation of papyrus and a great talent for the manufacture of stone vessels, to which they brought a beauty of design that is not excelled today. They also made an almost unlimited range of stone and copper tools, from saws to the finest needles. Their decorative objects of wood, ivory and gold are masterly, and their manufacture of leather, textiles and rope was of a high standard. Above all they had great artistic ability: the motifs of painting and sculpture that were characteristic of Egypt for 3,000 years had already appeared.

it are many rooms for the storage of food and other goods. The long rows of small chambers on three sides of the tomb are the graves of retainers sacrificed to accompany the king.

This advanced civilization appears suddenly in the early years of the third millennium B.C.; it seems to have little or no background in the Nile Valley. Yet the Valley had been inhabited for a long period before the First Dynasty. Excavation has indicated that during this period burial customs developed little; the passage of time is marked only by changes in the design of pottery and other objects. The people of the period had an advanced neolithic culture which certainly made a contribution to the later Egyptian civilization. In my opinion, however, their culture does not pro-

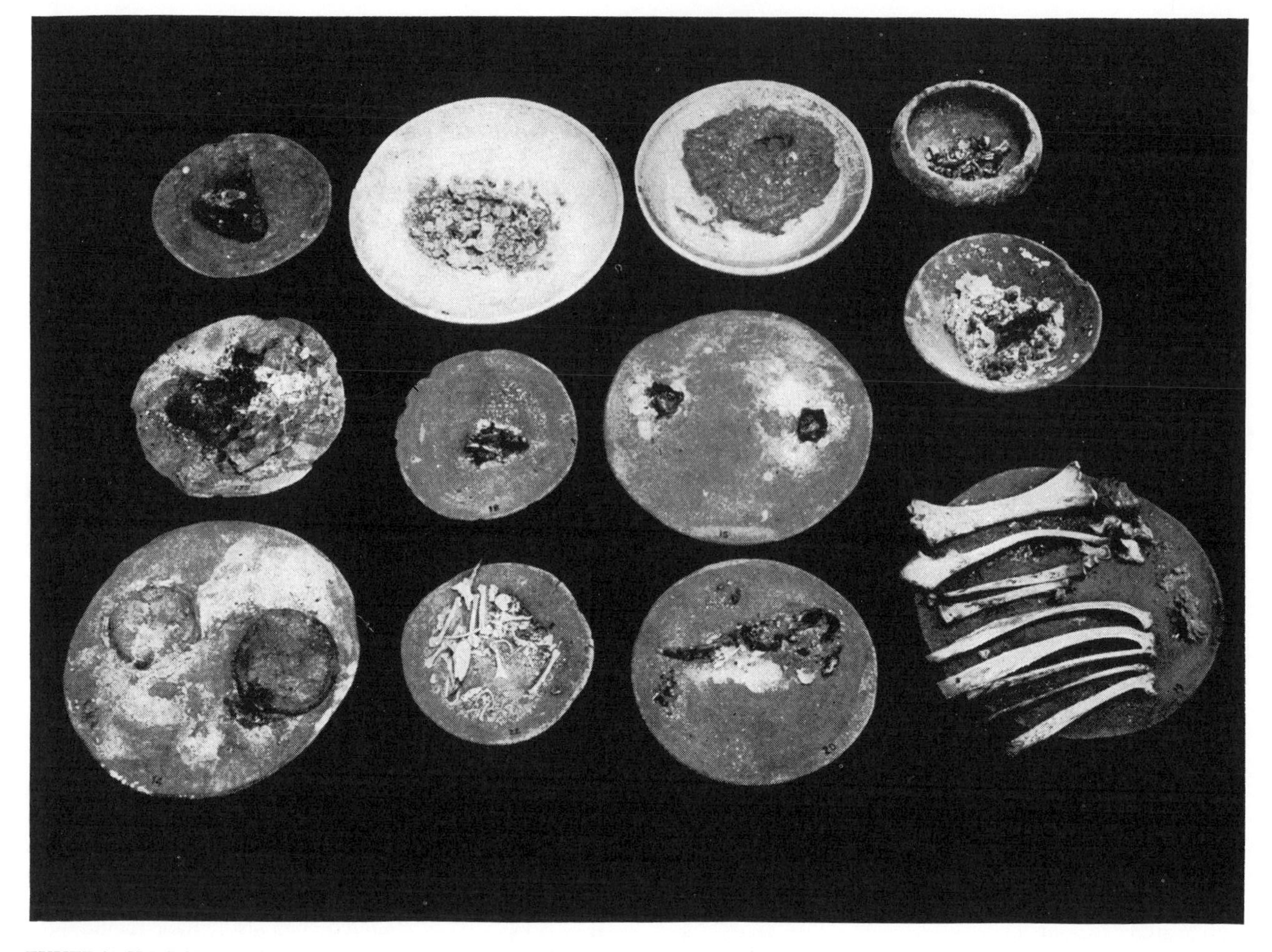

FUNERARY MEAL found in a tomb of the early Second Dynasty is in a remarkable state of preservation, considering that it was set out some 5,000 years ago. Fragments found in tombs of the First Dynasty indicate that similar meals were buried with its pharaohs.

vide a complete foundation for the Egypt of the pharaohs. It is of course possible that the architecture of the First Dynasty was the product of a superior people inhabiting the delta of the Nile, where constant flooding and agriculture has destroyed all remains of the period before the pharaohs. Since there is no evidence for or against this theory, it must remain speculative. In any case I feel it is unlikely that such a civilization could develop independently in the marshlands of the delta and suddenly impose itself on the upper Nile Valley. It is significant that during the First Dynasty only the nobles and officials were buried in monumental tombs. The mass of the people were buried in graves consisting of shallow pits with no superstructure beyond a circular mound of earth. The body lay in a huddled position on its left side; except for the objects in it such a grave had little to distinguish it from those of the period before the First Dynasty. By the end of the Second Dynasty we find the mass of the people had adopted the burial customs of their betters: the design of their tombs was the same in almost every detail except size. All this plainly suggests the existence of a superior culture which gradually imposed its burial customs on the conquered indigenes.

If we accept the theory that the civilization of the pharaohs was brought to the Nile Valley by a new people, we must ask: Who were they and where did they come from? The British historian Reginald Engelbach suggested a horde invasion, and there is evidence to suggest something of the sort. We must not overlook, however, the possibility of gradual infiltration over a long period. The monumental architecture of the First Dynasty has been compared to that of the Jemdet Nasr period in Mesopotamia, and I think the similarity is beyond dispute. But there are also great differences, so a direct connection between the Euphrates and the Nile at that time is still a matter of doubt. Thus the problem of how the civilization of the pharaohs originated remains unsolved. It is to be hoped that the further work of the Egypt Exploration Society will contribute to its solution.

Teotihuacán

7

by René Millon
June 1967

The first and largest city of the pre-Columbian New World arose in the Valley of Mexico during the first millenium A.D. At its height the metropolis covered a larger area than imperial Rome

When the Spaniards conquered Mexico, they described Montezuma's capital Tenochtitlán in such vivid terms that for centuries it seemed that the Aztec stronghold must have been the greatest city of pre-Columbian America. Yet only 25 miles to the north of Tenochtitlán was the site of a city that had once been even more impressive. Known as Teotihuacán, it had risen, flourished and fallen hundreds of years before the conquistadors entered Mexico. At the height of its power, around A.D. 500, Teotihuacán was larger than imperial Rome. For more than half a millennium it was to Middle America what Rome, Benares or Mecca have been to the Old World: at once a religious and cultural capital and a major economic and political center.

Unlike many of the Maya settlements to the south, in both Mexico and Guatemala, Teotihuacán was never a "lost" city. The Aztecs were still worshiping at its sacred monuments at the time of the Spanish Conquest, and scholarly studies of its ruins have been made since the middle of the 19th century. Over the past five years, however, a concerted program of investigation has yielded much new information about this early American urban center.

In the Old World the first civilizations were associated with the first cities, but both in Middle America and in Peru the rise of civilization does not seem to have occurred in an urban setting. As far as we can tell today, the foundation for the earliest civilization in Middle America was laid in the first millennium B.C. by a people we know as the Olmecs. None of the major Olmec centers discovered so far is a city. Instead these centers—the most important of which are located in the forested lowlands along the Gulf of Mexico on the narrow Isthmus of Tehuantepec—were of a ceremonial character, with small permanent populations probably consisting of priests and their attendants.

The Olmecs and those who followed them left to many other peoples of Middle America, among them the builders of Teotihuacán, a heritage of religious beliefs, artistic symbolism and other cultural traditions. Only the Teotihuacanos, however, created an urban civilization of such vigor that it significantly influenced the subsequent development of most other Middle American civilizations—urban and nonurban—down to the time of the Aztecs. It is hard to say exactly why this happened, but at least some of the contributing factors are evident. The archaeological record suggests the following sequence of events.

A settlement of moderate size existed at Teotihuacán fairly early in the first century B.C. At about the same time a number of neighboring religious centers were flourishing. One was Cuicuilco, to the southwest of Teotihuacán in the Valley of Mexico; another was Cholula, to the east in the Valley of Puebla. The most important influences shaping the "Teotihuacán way" probably stemmed from centers such as these. Around the time of Christ, Teotihuacán began to grow rapidly, and between A.D. 100 and 200 its largest religious monument was raised on the site of an earlier shrine. Known today as the Pyramid of the Sun, it was as large at the base as the great pyramid of Cheops in Egypt [*see bottom illustration on page 92*].

The powerful attraction of a famous holy place is not enough, of course, to explain Teotihuacán's early growth or later importance. The city's strategic location was one of a number of material factors that contributed to its rise. Teotihuacán lies astride the narrow waist of a valley that is the best route between the Valley of Mexico and the Valley of Puebla. The Valley of Puebla, in turn, is the gateway to the lowlands along the Gulf of Mexico.

The lower part of Teotihuacán's valley is a rich alluvial plain, watered by permanent springs and thus independent of the uncertainties of highland rainfall. The inhabitants of the valley seem early to have dug channels to create an irrigation system and to provide their growing city with water. Even today a formerly swampy section at the edge of the ancient city is carved by channels into "chinampas": small artificial islands that are intensively farmed. Indeed, it is possible that this form of agriculture, which is much better known as it was practiced in Aztec times near Tenochtitlán, was invented centuries earlier by the people of Teotihuacán.

The valley had major deposits of obsidian, the volcanic glass used all over ancient Middle America to make cutting and scraping tools and projectile points. Obsidian mining in the valley was apparently most intensive during the city's early years. Later the Teotihuacanos appear to have gained control of deposits of obsidian north of the Valley of Mexico that were better suited than the local material to the mass production of blade implements. Trade in raw obsidian and obsidian implements became increasingly important to the economy of Teotihuacán, reaching a peak toward the middle of the first millennium A.D.

The recent investigation of Teotihuacán has been carried forward by specialists working on three independent but related projects. One project was a monumental program of excavation and reconstruction undertaken by Mexico's National Institute of Anthropology, headed by Eusebio Dávalos. From 1962 to 1964 archaeologists under the direction of Ignacio Bernal, director of the

National Museum of Anthropology, unearthed and rebuilt a number of the structures that lie along the city's principal avenue ("the Street of the Dead"); they have also restored Teotihuacán's second main pyramid ("the Pyramid of the Moon"), which lies at the avenue's northern end. Two of the city's four largest structures, the Pyramid of the Sun and the Citadel, within which stands the Temple of Quetzalcoatl, had been cleared and restored in the 1900's and the 1920's respectively. Among other notable achievements, the National Institute's work brought to light some of the city's finest mural paintings.

As the Mexican archaeologists were at work a group under the direction of William T. Sanders of Pennsylvania State University conducted an intensive study of the ecology and the rural-settlement patterns of the valley. Another group, from the University of Rochester, initiated a mapping project under my direction. This last effort, which is still under way, involves preparing a detailed topographic map on which all the city's several thousand structures will be located. The necessary information is being secured by the examination of surface remains, supplemented by small-scale excavations. One result of our work has been to demonstrate how radically different Teotihuacán was from all other settlements of its time in Middle America. It was here that the New World's urban revolution exploded into being.

It had long been clear that the center of Teotihuacán was planned, but it soon became apparent to us that the extent and magnitude of the planning went far beyond the center. Our mapping revealed that the city's streets and the large majority of its buildings had been laid out along the lines of a precise grid aligned with the city center. The grid was established in Teotihuacán's formative days, but it may have been more intensively exploited later, perhaps in relation to "urban renewal" projects undertaken when the city had become rich and powerful.

The prime direction of the grid is slightly east of north (15.5 degrees). The basic modular unit of the plan is close to 57 meters. A number of residential structures are squares of this size. The plan of many of the streets seems to repeat various multiples of the 57-meter unit. The city's major avenues, which run parallel to the north-south axis, are spaced at regular intervals. Even the river running through the center of the city was canalized to conform to the grid. Miles from the city center the remains of buildings are oriented to the grid, even when they were built on slopes that ran counter to it. A small design composed of concentric circles divided into quadrants may have served as a standard surveyor's mark; it is sometimes pecked into the floors of buildings and sometimes into bare bedrock. One such pair of marks two miles apart forms a line

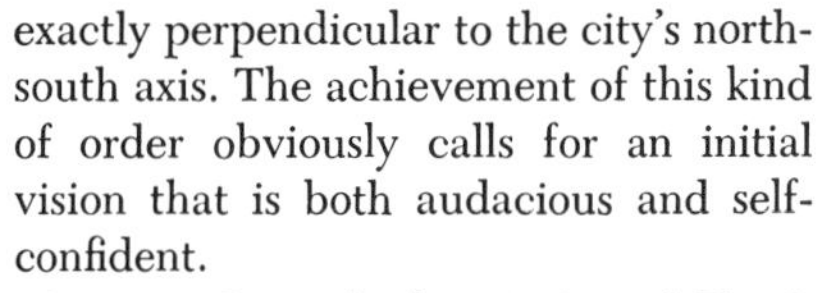

exactly perpendicular to the city's north-south axis. The achievement of this kind of order obviously calls for an initial vision that is both audacious and self-confident.

A city planner's description of Teotihuacán would begin not with the monumental Pyramid of the Sun but with the two complexes of structures that form the city center. These are the Citadel and the Great Compound, lying respectively to the. east and west of the city's main north-south avenue, the Street of the Dead. The names given the various structures and features of Teotihuacán are not, incidentally, the names by which the Teotihuacanos knew them. Some come from Spanish translations of Aztec names; others were bestowed by earlier archaeologists or by our mappers and are often the place names used by the local people.

The Street of the Dead forms the main axis of the city. At its northern end it stops at the Pyramid of the Moon, and

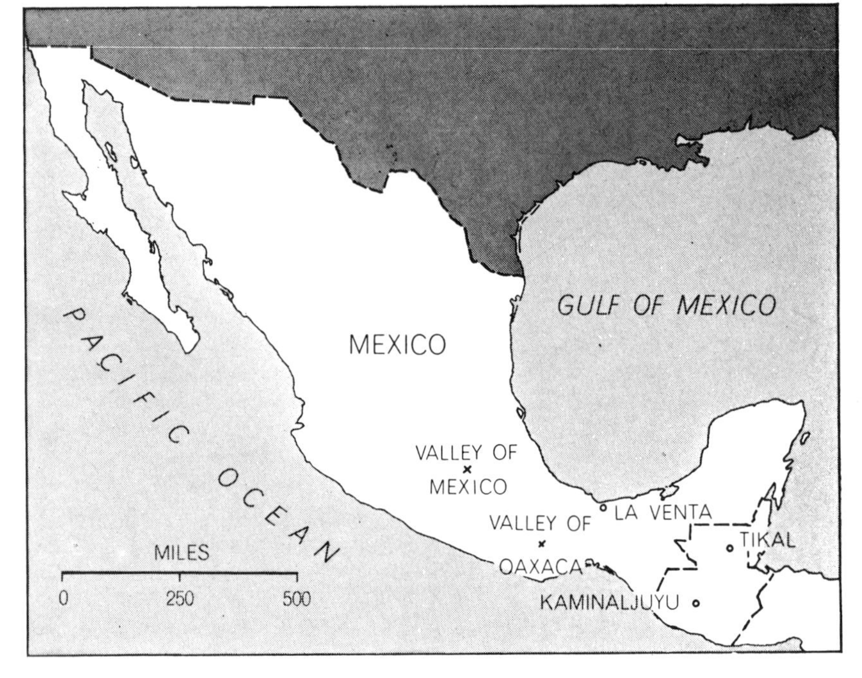

EARLY CIVILIZATION in Middle America appeared first in the lowlands along the Gulf of Mexico at such major centers of Olmec culture as La Venta. Soon thereafter a number of ceremonial centers appeared in the highlands, particularly in the valleys of Oaxaca, Puebla and Mexico. Kaminaljuyu and Tikal, Maya centers respectively in highlands and lowlands of what is now Guatemala, came under Teotihuacán's influence at the height of its power.

CEREMONIAL HEART of Teotihuacán is seen in an aerial photograph looking southeast toward Cerro Patlachique, one of a pair of mountains that flank the narrow valley dominated by the city. The large pyramid in

we have found that to the south it extends for two miles beyond the Citadel-Compound complex. The existence of a subordinate axis running east and west had not been suspected until our mappers discovered one broad avenue running more than two miles to the east of the Citadel and a matching avenue extending the same distance westward from the Compound.

To make it easier to locate buildings over so large an area we imposed our own 500-meter grid on the city, orienting it to the Street of the Dead and using the center of the city as the zero point of the system [*see bottom illustration, p. 91*]. The heavy line defining the limits of the city was determined by walking around the perimeter of the city and examining evidence on the surface to establish where its outermost remains end. The line traces a zone free of such remains that is at least 300 meters wide and that sharply separates the city from the countryside. The Street of the Dead, East Avenue and West Avenue divide Teotihuacán into quadrants centered on the Citadel-Compound complex. We do not know if these were formally recognized as administrative quarters of the city, as they were in Tenochtitlán. It is nonetheless possible that they may have been, since there are a number of other similarities between the two cities.

Indeed, during the past 25 years Mexican scholars have argued for a high degree of continuity in customs and beliefs from the Aztecs back to the Teotihuacanos, based partly on an assumed continuity in language. This hypothetical continuity, which extends through the intervening Toltec times, provides valuable clues in interpreting archaeological evidence. For example, the unity of religion and politics that archaeologists postulate at Teotihuacán is reinforced by what is known of Aztec society.

The public entrance of the Citadel is a monumental staircase on the Street of the Dead. Inside the Citadel a plaza opens onto the Temple of Quetzalcoatl, the principal sacred building in this area. The temple's façade represents the most successful integration of architecture and sculpture so far discovered at Teotihuacán [*see bottom illustration on page 94*].

The Great Compound, across the street from the Citadel, had gone unrecognized as a major structure until our survey. We found that it differs from all other known structures at Teotihuacán and that in area it is the city's largest. Its main components are two great raised platforms. These form a north and a south wing and are separated by broad entrances at the level of the street on the east and west. The two wings thus flank a plaza somewhat larger than the one within the Citadel. Few of the structures on the platforms seem to have been temples or other religious buildings. Most of them face away from the Street of the Dead, whereas almost all the other known structures along the avenue face toward it.

the foreground is the Pyramid of the Moon. The larger one beyond it is the Pyramid of the Sun. Many of the more than 100 smaller religious structures that line the city's central avenue, the Street of the Dead, are visible in the photograph. South of the Pyramid of the Sun and east of the central avenue is the large enclosure known as the Citadel. It and the Great Compound, a matching structure not visible in the photograph, formed the city's center. More than 4,000 additional buildings, most no longer visible, spread for miles beyond the center. At the peak of Teotihuacán's power, around A.D. 500, the population of the city was more than 50,000.

One therefore has the impression that the Compound was not devoted to religious affairs. In the Citadel there are clusters of rooms to the north and south of the Temple of Quetzalcoatl, but the overall effect conveyed by the temples and the other buildings that surround the Citadel's plaza is one of a political center in a sacred setting. Perhaps some of its rooms housed the high priests of Teotihuacán.

The plaza of the Compound is a strategically located open space that could have been the city's largest marketplace. The buildings that overlook this plaza could have been at least partly devoted to the administration of the economic affairs of the city. Whatever their functions were, the Citadel and the Compound are the heart of the city. Together they form a majestic spatial unit,

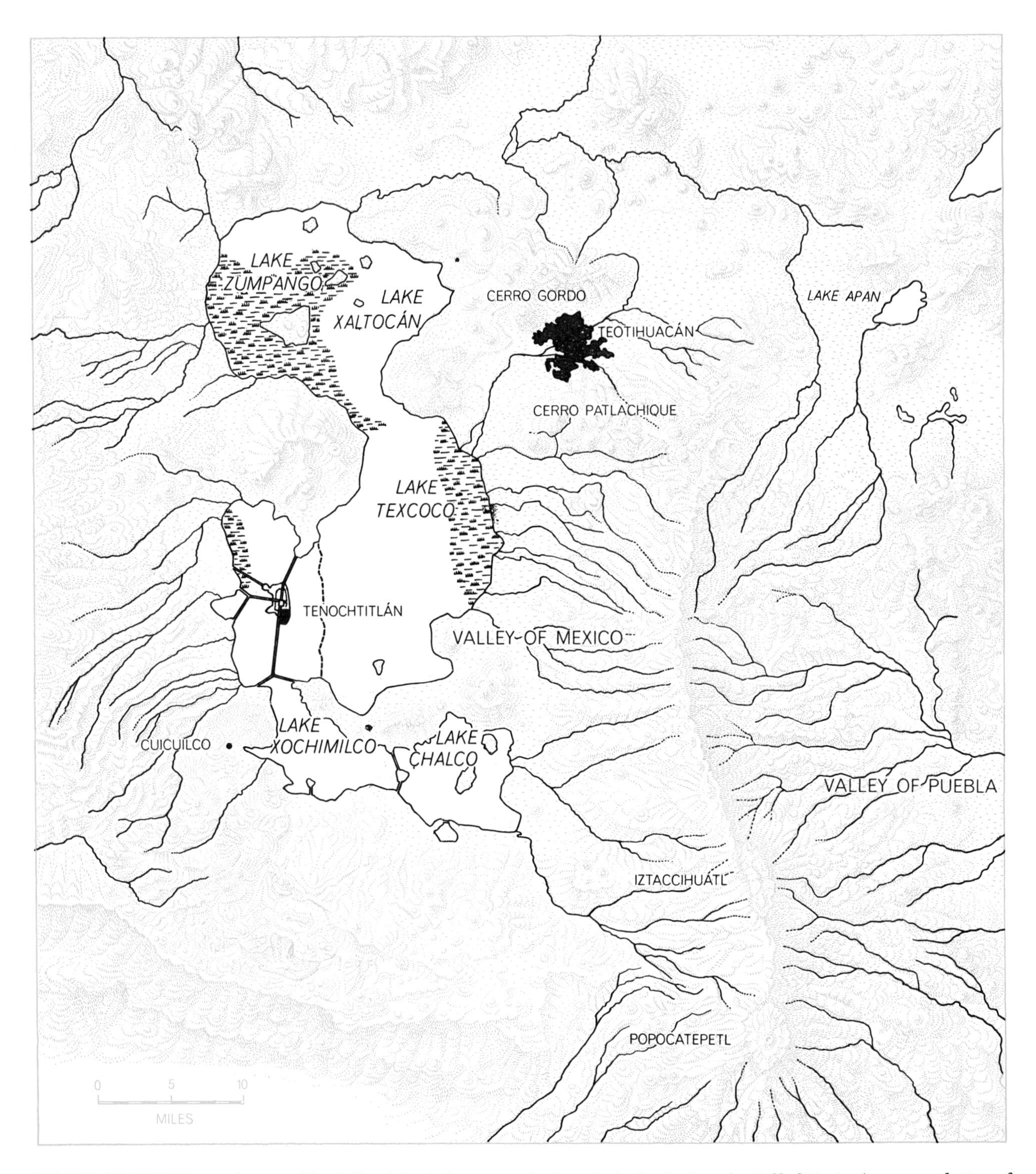

VALLEY OF MEXICO was dominated by shallow lakes in late pre-Hispanic times; in the rainy season they coalesced into a single body of water. Teotihuacán was strategically located; it commanded a narrow valley a few miles northeast of the lakes that provided the best route between the Valley of Mexico and the Valley of Puebla, which leads to the lowlands along the Gulf of Mexico (*see map at bottom of page 86*). It was an important center of trade and worship from 100 B.C. until about A.D. 750. Centuries after its fall the Aztec capital of Tenochtitlán grew up in the western shallows of Lake Texcoco, 25 miles from the earlier metropolis.

a central island surrounded by more open ground than is found in any other part of Teotihuacán.

The total area of the city was eight square miles. Not counting ritual structures, more than 4,000 buildings, most of them apartment houses, were built to shelter the population. At the height of Teotihuacán's power, in the middle of the first millennium A.D., the population certainly exceeded 50,000 and was probably closer to 100,000. This is not a particularly high figure compared with Old World religious-political centers; today the population of Mecca is some 130,000 and that of Benares more than 250,000 (to which is added an annual influx of a million pilgrims). One reason Teotihuacán did not have a larger population was that its gleaming lime-plastered residential structures were only

APARTMENT HOUSE typical of the city's many multiroomed dwellings was excavated in 1961 by Laurette Séjourné. The outer walls of the compound conform with the 57-meter module favored by the city's planners. Within its forbidding exterior (*see south façade at bottom of illustration*) individual apartments comprised several rooms grouped around unroofed patios (*smaller white areas*).

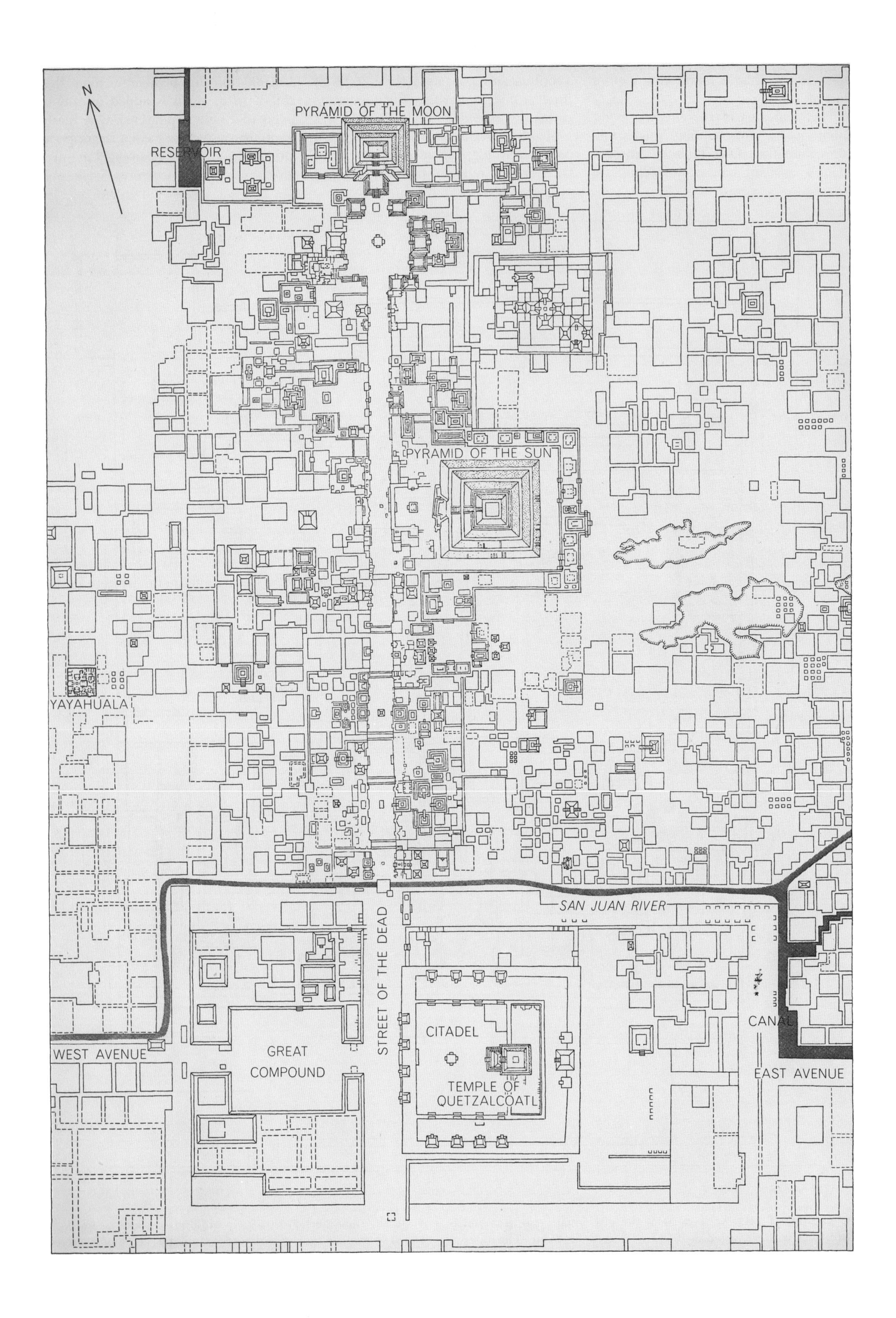
N
PYRAMID OF THE MOON
RESERVOIR
PYRAMID OF THE SUN
YAYAHUALA
SAN JUAN RIVER
STREET OF THE DEAD
CANAL
WEST AVENUE
GREAT
COMPOUND
CITADEL
TEMPLE OF
QUETZALCOATL
EAST AVENUE

one story high. Although most of the inhabitants lived in apartments, the buildings were "ranch-style" rather than "high-rise."

The architects of Teotihuacán designed apartments to offer a maximum of privacy within the crowded city, using a concept similar to the Old World's classical atrium house [*see illustration on page 89*]. The rooms of each apartment surrounded a central patio; each building consisted of a series of rooms, patios, porticoes and passageways, all secluded from the street. This pattern was also characteristic of the city's palaces. The residential areas of Teotihuacán must have presented a somewhat forbidding aspect from the outside: high windowless walls facing on narrow streets. Within the buildings, however, the occupants were assured of privacy. Each patio had its own drainage system; each admitted light and air to the surrounding apartments; each made it possible for the inhabitants to be out of doors yet alone. It may be that this architectural style contributed to Teotihuacán's permanence as a focus of urban life for more than 500 years.

The basic building materials of Teotihuacán were of local origin. Outcrops of porous volcanic rock in the valley were quarried and the stone was crushed and mixed with lime and earth to provide a kind of moisture-resistant concrete that was used as the foundation for floors and walls. The same material was used for roofing; wooden posts spaced at intervals bore much of the weight of the roof. Walls were made of stone and mortar or of sunbaked adobe brick. Floors and wall surfaces were then usually finished with highly polished plaster.

What kinds of people lived in Teotihuacán? Religious potentates, priestly bureaucrats and military leaders presumably occupied the top strata of the city's society, but their number could not have been large. Many of the inhabitants tilled lands outside the city and many others must have been artisans: potters, workers in obsidian and stone and craftsmen dealing with more perishable materials such as cloth, leather, feathers and wood (traces of which are occasionally preserved). Well-defined concentrations of surface remains suggest that craft groups such as potters and workers in stone and obsidian tended to live together in their own neighborhoods. This lends weight to the hypothesis that each apartment building was solely occupied by a "corporate" group, its families related on the basis of occupation, kinship or both. An arrangement of this kind, linking the apartment dwellers to one another by webs of joint interest and activity, would have promoted social stability.

If groups with joint interests lived not only in the same apartment building but also in the same general neighborhood, the problem of governing the city would have been substantially simplified. Such organization of neighborhood groups could have provided an intermediate level between the individual and the state. Ties of cooperation, competition or even conflict between people in different neighborhoods could have created the kind of social network that is favorable to cohesion.

The marketplace would similarly have made an important contribution to the integration of Teotihuacán society. If the greater part of the exchange of goods and services in the city took place in one or more major markets (such as the one that may have occupied the plaza of the Great Compound), then not only the Teotihuacanos but also the outsiders who used the markets would have felt a vested interest in maintaining "the peace of the market." Moreover, the religion of Teotihuacán would have imbued the city's economic institutions with a sacred quality.

The various social groups in the city left some evidence of their identity. For example, we located a walled area, associated with the west side of the Pyramid of the Moon, where large quantities of waste obsidian suggest that obsidian workers may have formed part of a larger temple community. We also found what looks like a foreign neighborhood. Occupied by people who apparently came to Teotihuacán from the Valley of Oaxaca, the area lies in the western part of the city. It is currently under study by

CITY CENTER is composed of two sets of structures, the Great Compound and the Citadel (*bottom illustration on opposite page*). They stand on either side of the Street of the Dead, the main north-south axis of the city. A pair of avenues approaching the center of the city from east and west form the secondary axis. The city's largest religious monuments were the Pyramid of the Sun, the Pyramid of the Moon and the Temple of Quetzalcoatl, which lies inside the Citadel. Yayahuala (*left of center*) was one of many residential compounds. Its architecture is shown in detail on page 89.

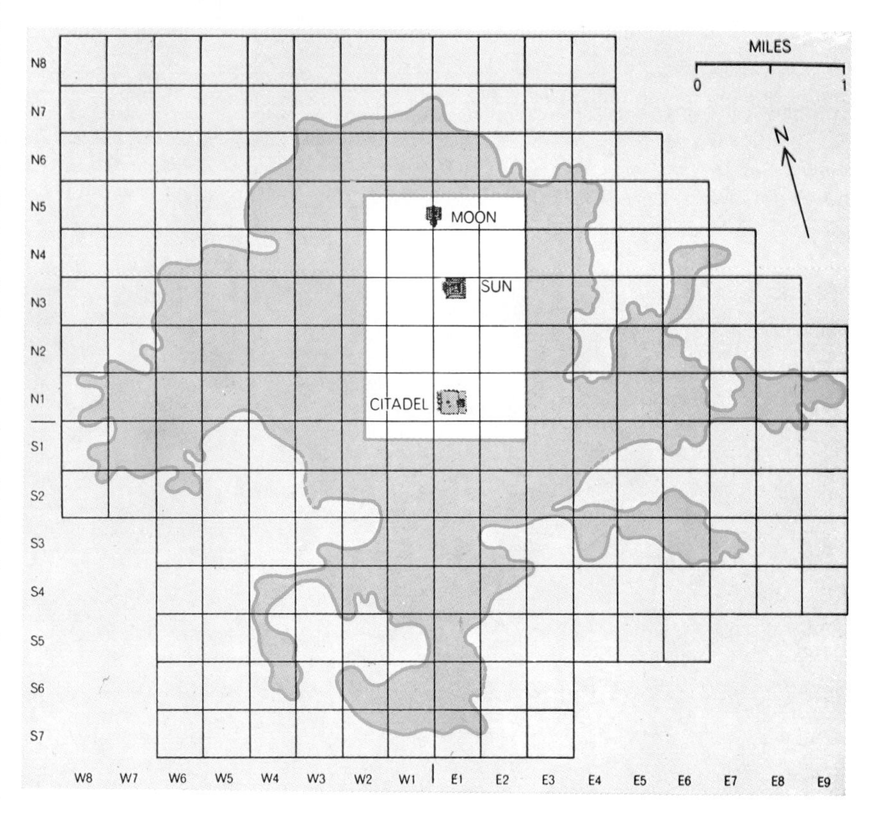

IRREGULAR BOUNDARY of Teotihuacán is shown by a solid line that approaches the edges of a grid, composed of 500-meter squares, surveyed by the author's team. The grid parallels the north-south direction of the Street of the Dead, the city's main avenue. One extension of the city in its early period, which is only partly known, has been omitted. A map of Teotihuacán's north-central zone (*light color*) is reproduced on page 90.

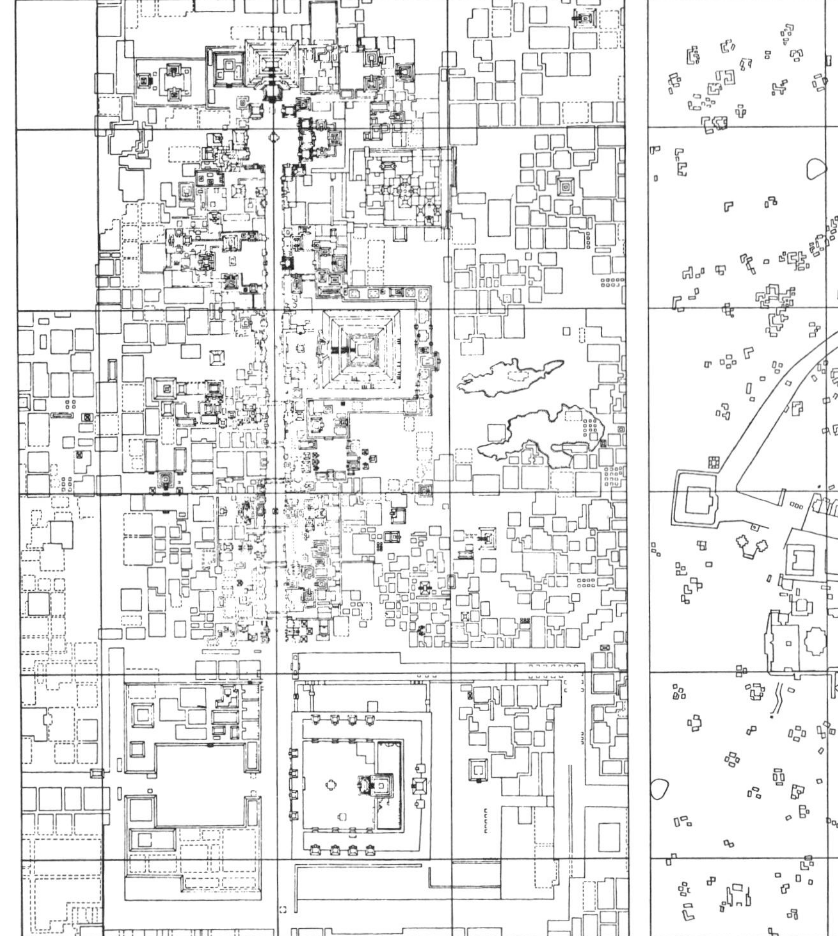

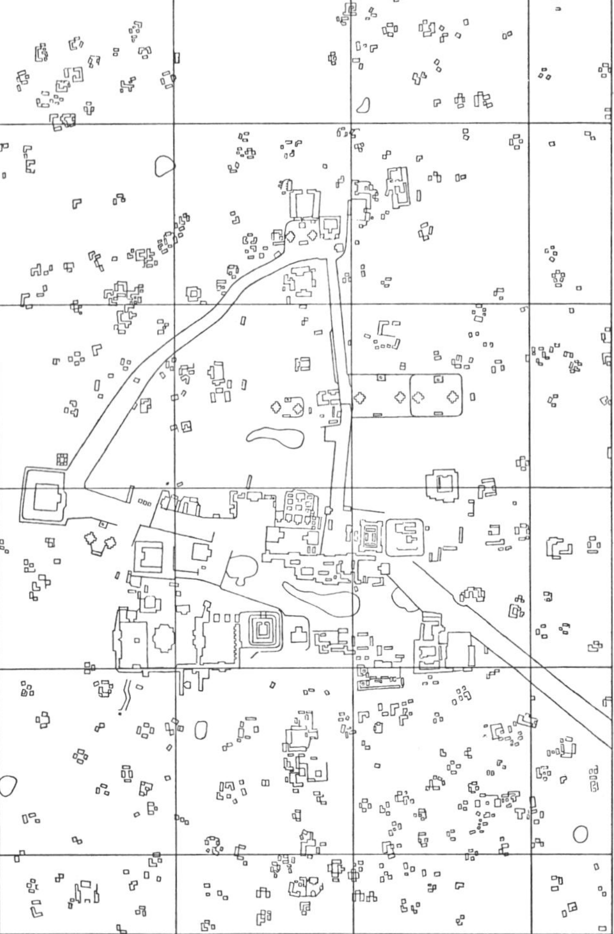

DENSITY OF SETTLEMENT at Teotihuacán is compared with that at Tikal, largest of the lowland Maya ceremonial centers in Middle America. The maps show the central area of each settlement at the same scale. The data for Teotihuacán (*left*) are from surveys by the author and the Mexican government. Those for Tikal (*right*) are from a survey by the University of Pennsylvania. Even though its center included many public structures, Teotihuacán's concentrated residential pattern shows its urban character.

PYRAMID OF THE SUN is as broad at the base as the great pyramid of Cheops in Egypt, although it is only half as high. It was built over the site of an earlier shrine during Teotihuacán's first major period of growth, in the early centuries of the Christian era.

John Paddock of the University of the Americas, a specialist in the prehistory of Oaxaca. Near the eastern edge of the city quantities of potsherds have been found that are characteristic of Maya areas and the Veracruz region along the Gulf of Mexico. These fragments suggest that the neighborhood was inhabited either by people from those areas or by local merchants who specialized in such wares.

We have found evidence that as the centuries passed two of the city's important crafts—the making of pottery and obsidian tools—became increasingly specialized. From the third century A.D. on some obsidian workshops contain a high proportion of tools made by striking blades from a "core" of obsidian; others have a high proportion of tools made by chipping a piece of obsidian until the desired shape was obtained. Similar evidence of specialization among potters is found in the southwestern part of the city. There during Teotihuacán's period of greatest expansion one group of potters concentrated on the mass production of the most common type of cooking ware.

The crafts of Teotihuacán must have helped to enrich the city. So also, no doubt, did the pilgrim traffic. In addition to the three major religious structures more than 100 other temples and shrines line the Street of the Dead. Those who visited the city's sacred buildings must have included not only peasants and townspeople from the entire Valley of Mexico but also pilgrims from as far away as Guatemala. When one adds to these worshipers the visiting merchants, traders and peddlers attracted by the markets of Teotihuacán, it seems likely that many people would have been occupied catering to the needs of those who were merely visiting the city.

Radical social transformations took place during the growth of the city. As Teotihuacán increased in size there was first a relative and then an absolute decline in the surrounding rural population. This is indicated by both our data from the city and Sanders' from the countryside. Apparently many rural populations left their villages and were concentrated in the city. The process seems to have accelerated around A.D. 500, when the population of the city approached its peak. Yet the marked increase in density within the city was accompanied by a reduction in the city's size. It was at this time, during the sixth century, that urban renewal programs may have been undertaken in areas

HUMAN FIGURE, wearing a feather headdress, face paint and sandals, decorates the side of a vase dating from the sixth century A.D. Similar figures often appear in the city's murals.

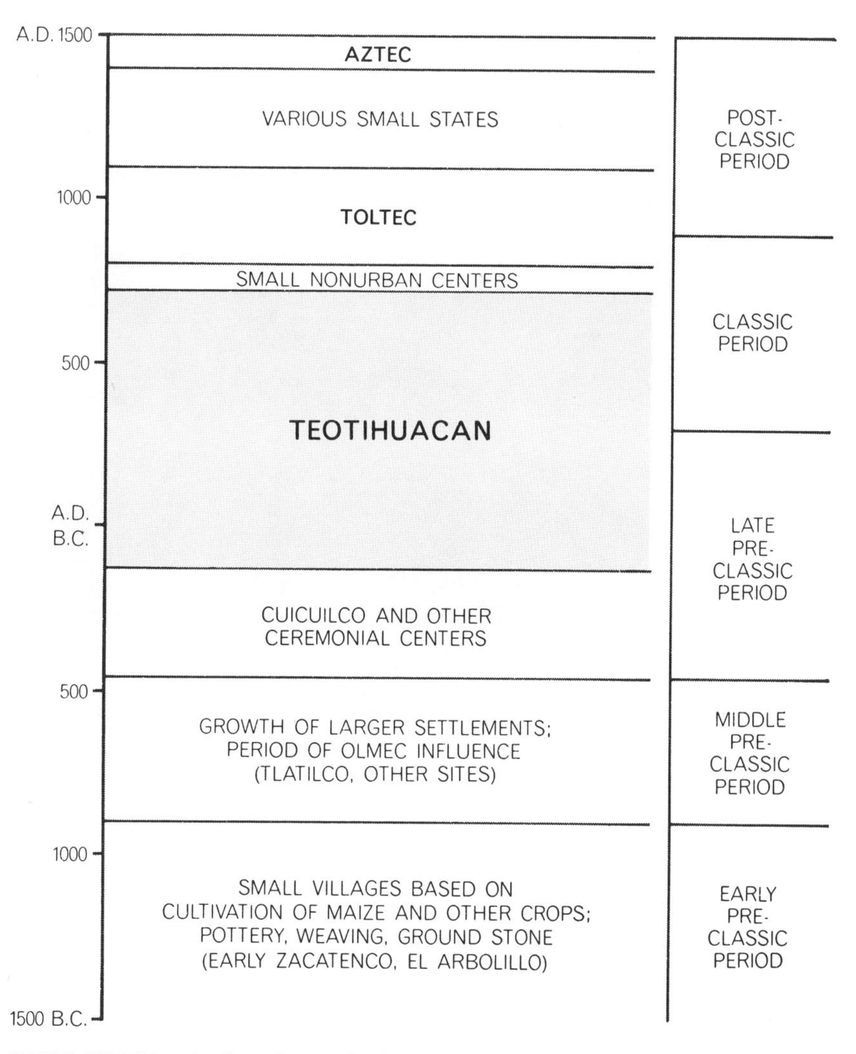

CITY'S BIRTH took place during the late pre-Classic Period in the Valley of Mexico, about a century before the beginning of the Christian era. Other highland ceremonial centers such as Cuicuilco in the Valley of Mexico and Cholula in the Valley of Puebla were influential at that time. Although Teotihuacán fell in about A.D. 750, near the end of the Classic Period, its religious monuments were deemed sacred by the Aztecs until Hispanic times.

PYRAMID OF THE MOON, excavated in the early 1960's by a Mexican government group under the direction of Ignacio Bernal, stands at the northern end of the Street of the Dead. The façade presented to the avenue (*above*) consists of several interlocking, truncated pyramids thrusting toward the sky. The structure, 150 feet high and 490 feet wide at the base, is smaller than the Pyramid of the Sun but is architecturally more sophisticated.

TEMPLE OF QUETZALCOATL is the major religious structure within the Citadel, the eastern half of Teotihuacán's city center. The building is believed to represent the most successful integration of sculpture and architecture to be achieved throughout the city's long history. A covering layer of later construction protected the ornate facade from damage.

where density was on the rise.

Such movements of rural and urban populations must have conflicted with local interests. That they were carried out successfully demonstrates the prestige and power of the hierarchy in Teotihuacán. Traditional loyalties to the religion of Teotihuacán were doubtless invoked. Nevertheless, one wonders if the power of the military would not have been increasingly involved. There is evidence both in Teotihuacán and beyond its borders that its soldiers became more and more important from the fifth century on. It may well be that at the peak of its power and influence Teotihuacán itself was becoming an increasingly oppressive place in which to live.

The best evidence of the power and influence that the leaders of Teotihuacán exercised elsewhere in Middle America comes from Maya areas. One ancient religious center in the Maya highlands—Kaminaljuyu, the site of modern Guatemala City—appears to have been occupied at one time by priests and soldiers from Teotihuacán. Highland Guatemala received a massive infusion of Teotihuacán cultural influences, with Teotihuacán temple architecture replacing older styles. This has been recognized for some time, but only recently has it become clear that Teotihuacán also influenced the Maya lowlands. The people of Tikal in Guatemala, largest of the lowland Maya centers, are now known to have been under strong influence from Teotihuacán. The people of Tikal adopted some of Teotihuacán's artistic traditions and erected a massive stone monument to Teotihuacán's rain god. William R. Coe of the University of Pennsylvania and his colleagues, who are working at Tikal, are in the midst of evaluating the nature and significance of this influence.

Tikal provides an instructive measure of the difference in the density of construction in Maya population centers and those in central Mexico. It was estimated recently that Tikal supported a population of about 10,000. As the illustration at the top of page 92 shows, the density of Teotihuacán's central area is strikingly different from that of Tikal's. Not only was Teotihuacán's population at least five times larger than Tikal's but also it was far less dispersed. In such a crowded urban center problems of integration, cohesion and social control must have been of a totally different order of magnitude than those of a less populous and less compact ceremonial center such as Tikal.

What were the circumstances of Teotihuacán's decline and fall? Almost certainly both environmental and social factors were involved. The climate of the region is semiarid today, and there is evidence that a long-term decline in annual rainfall brought the city to a similar condition in the latter half of the first millennium A.D. Even before then deforestation of the surrounding hills may have begun a process of erosion that caused a decrease in the soil moisture available for crops. Although persistent drought would have presented increasingly serious problems for those who fed the city, this might have been the lesser of its consequences. More ominous would have been the effect of increasing aridity on the cultivators of marginal lands and the semisedentary tribesmen in the highlands north of the Valley of Mexico. As worsening conditions forced these peoples to move, the Teotihuacanos might have found themselves not only short of food but also under military pressure along their northern frontier.

Whether or not climatic change was a factor, some signs of decline—such as the lowering of standards of construction and pottery-making—are evident during the last century of Teotihuacán's existence. Both a reduction in population and a tendency toward dispersion suggest that the fabric of society was suffering from strains and weaknesses. Once such a process of deterioration passed a critical point the city would have become vulnerable to attack.

No evidence has been found that Teotihuacán as a whole had formal defenses. Nonetheless, the valley's drainage pattern provides some natural barriers, large parts of the city were surrounded by walls or massive platforms and its buildings were formidable ready-made fortresses. Perhaps the metropolis was comparatively unprotected because it had for so long had an unchallenged supremacy.

In any case, archaeological evidence indicates that around A.D. 750 much of central Teotihuacán was looted and burned, possibly with the help of the city's own people. The repercussions of Teotihuacán's fall seem to have been felt throughout civilized Middle America. The subsequent fall of Monte Alban, the capital of the Oaxaca region, and of many Maya ceremonial centers in Guatemala and the surrounding area may reasonably be associated with dislocations set in motion by the fall of Teotihuacán. Indeed, the appropriate epitaph for the New World's first major metropolis may be that it was as influential in its collapse as in its long and brilliant flowering.

FEATHERED SERPENT, from one of the earlier murals found at Teotihuacán, has a free, flowing appearance. The animal below the serpent is a jaguar; the entire mural, which is not shown, was probably painted around A.D. 400. It may portray a cyclical myth of creation and destruction. The city's principal gods were often represented in the form of animals.

LATER SERPENT GOD, with a rattlesnake tail, is from a mural probably painted less than a century before the fall of Teotihuacán. The figure is rendered in a highly formal manner. A trend toward formalism is apparent in the paintings produced during the city's final years.

BIBLIOGRAPHIES

I THE CHANGING NATURE OF ANTHROPOLOGICAL ARCHAEOLOGY

1. The Hopewell Cult

EXPLORATION OF THE MOUND CITY GROUP. William C. Mills in *Ohio Archaeological and Historical Quarterly*, Vol. 31, No. 4, pages 423–584; October, 1922.

EXPLORATIONS OF THE SEIP GROUP OF PRE-HISTORIC EARTHWORKS. Henry C. Shetrone and Emerson F. Greenman in *Ohio Archaeological and Historical Quarterly,* Vol. 40, No. 3, pages 349–509; July, 1931.

II STONEHENGE

2. Stonehenge

THE AGE OF STONEHENGE. E. Herbert Stone in *The Nineteenth Century and After*, Vol. 95, pages 97–105; January-June, 1924.

3. Carbon 14 and the Prehistory of Europe

COLONIALISM AND MEGALITHISMUS. Colin Renfrew in *Antiquity*, Vol. 41, No. 164, pages 276–288; December, 1967.

THE AUTONOMY OF THE SOUTH-EAST EUROPEAN COPPER AGE. Colin Renfrew in *Proceedings of the Prehistoric Society*, Vol. 35, pages 12–47; 1969.

NOBEL SYMPOSIUM 12: RADIOCARBON VARIATIONS AND ABSOLUTE CHRONOLOGY. Edited by Ingrid U. Olsson. John Wiley & Sons, Inc., 1970.

THE TREE-RING CALIBRATION OF RADIOCARBON: AN ARCHAEOLOGICAL EVALUATION. Colin Renfrew in *Proceedings of the Prehistoric Society,* Vol. 36, pages 280–311; 1970.

4. Megalithic Monuments

STONEHENGE. R. J. C. Atkinson. Macmillan and Company, 1956.

THE MEGALITH BUILDERS OF WESTERN EUROPE. Glyn L. Daniel. Praeger Publishers, 1958.

BRITTANY. P. R. Giot. Praeger Publishers, 1960.

ANCIENT EUROPE FROM THE BEGINNINGS OF AGRICULTURE TO CLASSICAL ANTIQUITY. Stuart Piggott. Edinburgh University Press, 1965.

BEFORE CIVILIZATION: THE RADIOCARBON REVOLUTION AND PREHISTORIC EUROPE. Colin Renfrew. Alfred A. Knopf, Inc., 1973.

III LINES IN THE PERUVIAN DESERT

5. The Prehistoric Ground Drawings of Peru

ANCIENT DRAWINGS ON THE DESERT OF PERU. Paul Kosok and Maria Reiche in *Archaeology*, Vol. 2, No. 4, pages 206–215; December, 1949.

LIFE, LAND AND WATER IN ANCIENT PERU. Paul Kosok. Long Island University Press, 1965.

GIANT GROUND FIGURES OF THE PREHISTORIC DESERTS. Emma Lou Davis and Sylvia Winslow in *Proceedings of the American Philosophical Society*, Vol. 109, pages 8–21; 1965.

WAS HUARI A STATE? William H. Isbell and Katharina J. Schreiber in *American Antiquity*, Vol. 43, No. 3, pages 372–389; 1978.

IV PYRAMIDS

6. The Tombs of the First Pharaohs

GREAT TOMBS OF THE FIRST DYNASTY: EXCAVATIONS AT SAQQARA. Walter B. Emery. Vol. I, Government Press, 1949; Vol. II, Oxford University Press, 1954.

7. Teotihuacán

THE CULTURAL ECOLOGY OF THE TEOTIHUACÁN VALLEY. William T. Sanders. Department of Sociology and Anthropology, Pennsylvania State University, 1965.

INDIAN ART OF MEXICO AND CENTRAL AMERICA. Miguel Covarrubias. Alfred A. Knopf, Inc., 1957.

AN INTRODUCTION TO AMERICAN ARCHAEOLOGY, Vol. I: NORTH AND MIDDLE AMERICA. Gordon R. Willey. Prentice-Hall, Inc., 1969.

MESOAMERICA BEFORE THE TOLTECS. Wigberto Jiménez Moreno in *In Ancient Oaxaca*, edited by John Paddock. Stanford University Press, 1966.

MEXICO BEFORE CORTEZ: ART, HISTORY AND LEGEND. Ignacio Bernal. Doubleday & Company, Inc., 1963.

NORTHERN MESOAMERICA. Pedro Armillas in *Prehistoric Man in the New World*, edited by Jesse D. Jennings and Edward Norbeck. The University of Chicago Press, 1964.

INDEX

Abydos, 78, 83
Adena culture, 35
Agriculture. *See* Farming
Algeria, stone monuments in, 56
Altar Stone, at Stonehenge, 42, 43
Amélineau, Emile-Clément, 78
Ancient Egyptians, The (Smith), 56
Archaeology, vs. pseudoarchaeology, 1–24
Assam, stone monuments in, 56
Astronomical significance
  of megalithic monuments, 56
  of Nazca markings, 15–16, 75–76
  of pyramids, 22
  of Stonehenge, 11–13, 61
Atkinson, Richard, 8–10, 61, 63
Aubrey Holes, at Stonehenge, 10, 40–43
Aubrey, John, 65
Avebury, 39, 59, 65
Aveni, Anthony, 22
Avenue, at Stonehenge, 40, 41, 44
Aztec culture, 85–95

Badawy, Alexander, 19
Bergier, Jacques, 14, 17
Bernal, Ignacio, 85, 94
Bibby, Geoffrey, 8
Binford, Lewis R., 6
Blue stones, at Stonehenge, 12, 42, 43, 44, 61
Borchardt, Ludwig, 19
Bristlecone pine trees, for dating, 10, 50–55, 63
Brittany, megalithic monument in, 56, 57, 60–66
Brodgar, 59
Bronze Age, 47, 63
Bucha, V., 52
Burial sites
  European megaliths as, 47–55, 58–61, 63, 64
  of first pharaohs, 78–84
  Hopewell mounds as, 29–36
  pyramids as, 17–21
  at Stonehenge, 39, 40, 44
Burl, Aubrey, 12
Butzer, Karl, 20

Capstone, 59
Carbajal, Alberto, 76
Carbon-14 dating. *See* Radiocarbon dating
Carnac, megalithic monument at, 56, 57, 59
Carreg Samson cromlech, 60
Caucasus, stone monument in, 56
Cazeau, Charles J., 7
Chariots of the Gods? (Von Däniken), 14
Cheops, Great Pyramid of, 17–19
Childe, V. Gordon, 48–49, 54, 63
Cholula, 85
Christianity, and menhirs, 64–66
Citadel, 86–88, 91, 94
Clark, R. Malcolm, 63
Coe, William R., 94
Cole, John R., 7
Computers, aiding archaeologists, 3
"Copper Age," of Spain, 48, 49
Corbeled vaults, 48, 59
Corn, at Hopewell sites, 32, 33, 34
Crete, tombs of, 48, 49
Cuicuilco, 22, 85
Cultural diffusion. *See* Diffusion
Cultural evolutionary theory, 2
Culture. *See also* Diffusion
  archaeologists' view of, 2
  New World stages of, 35
  subsystems in, 2–3, 6–7
Cursus, at Stonehenge, 40
Cuzco, 16, 71, 73, 74
Cyclopean architecture, 56
Cyclops Christianus (Herbert), 56

Daniel, Glyn, 12, 48, 56–66
Dating techniques. *See* Bristlecone pine trees; Radiocarbon dating
Dávalos, Eusebio, 85
Dawn of European Civilisation (Childe), 48
Deer, at Hopewell site, 34
Diffusion
  dating techniques disproving, 47–55, 64
  vs. independent invention, 1, 2, 6, 10, 23, 32

Dolmen stone, 60

Economic uniformity, and Nazca drawings, 71, 73–74
Edwards, I.E.S., 20
Egypt
  pre-pyramid burial sites in, 78–84
  pyramids of, 1, 17–21
  and theory of cultural diffusion, 23, 47–48, 63
Egypt Exploration Society, 79, 84
El-Baz, Farouk, 20
Emery, Walter B., 19, 78–84
Engelbach, Reginald, 84
Erasmus, C.J., 12
Ethiopia, stone monuments in, 56
Europe. *See also* Stonehenge
  and carbon-14 dating, 47–55
  megalithic monuments in, 56–66
Exploring the Unknown (Cazeau and Scott), 7

Farming
  by Hopewell cult, 32–34
  and Nazca drawings, 71, 73
  signaling Neolithic period, 51
  in Teotihuacán valley, 85
Ferguson, Charles Wesley, 52
Fergusson, James, 8, 56
First Dynasty, in Egypt, 78–84
Firth, C.M., 78
Fort Ancient site, of Hopewell cult, 36
Fort Hill site, of Hopewell cult, 36
France, megalithic monuments in, 47, 59, 63, 64
Funeral customs. *See also* Burial sites
  of First Dynasty Egyptians, 79–80
  of Hopewell cult, 29–36

Geoffrey of Monmouth, 40
Geometry, Pythagorean, 61
Germany, stone monuments in, 59
Gingerich, Owen, 12
Gods from Outer Space (Von Däniken), 14
Gozo, 59, 62, 63
Grand Menhir Brisé, 56
Great Compound, 86–87, 91

Great Pyramid of Cheops, 17–19
Ground drawings, in Peru, 13–16, 69–76

Harness site, of Hopewell cult, 29, 32
Hawkes, Jacquetta, 8, 9, 39–45
Hawkins, Gerald, 11, 13, 15, 16, 61, 70, 75
Heel Stone, at Stonehenge, 10, 39
Hemaka (Egyptian noble), 79
Herbert, Algernon, 56
Hopewell cult, 3–6, 29–36
Hopewell, M.C., 29
Hor-Aha (Egyptian king), 81
Hoyle, Fred, 11
Huaca del Sol, 70
Huari, 71, 73, 76

Illinois, as Hopewell site, 29, 32, 33
Inca culture, 16, 71–76
India, stone monuments in, 56
Indians. *See* Aztec culture; Inca culture; Maya culture
Ireland, stone monuments in, 58, 59, 62–65
Iron Age, 47
Isbell, Billie Jean, 73, 75
Isbell, William, 13, 15, 69–76
Italy, stone monuments in, 59

Japan, stone monuments in, 56

Ka-a (Egyptian king), 79
Kaminaljuyu, 94
Kashmir, stone monuments in, 56
Knobloch, Patricia J., 73
Kosok, Paul, 14, 15, 16, 69
Kossinna, Gustaf, 48
Krupp, E.C., 11, 17, 19

Land, Life, and Water in Ancient Peru (Kosok), 15
Ley, Willy, 17, 19
Libby, Willard F., 9, 50, 61
Lockyer, Sir Norman, 11, 39, 61
Lumbreras, Luis, 15

McGraw, Alva, 33
McGraw site, of Hopewell cult, 32–35
MacKie, Euan, 11, 56
Maes Howe, 59, 64
Malta, stone temples of, 49, 59, 62, 63
Mastabas, 20
Maya culture, 1, 21, 24, 92–95
Megalith Builders, The (MacKie), 56
Megalithic Lunar Observatories (Thom), 61
Mendelssohn, Kurt, 17, 20–21, 23
Menhir, 56, 61, 63, 64, 66
Meryt-Nit (Egyptian Queen), 81
Mesoamerican pyramids, 1, 17, 21–23, 85–95
Mesopotamia, 47, 84
Mexico, Teotihuacán in, 1, 17, 21–23, 85–95
Mica, in Hopewell mounds, 29
Millon, René, 21, 22, 85–95
Milojčić, Vladimir, 51
Monte Alban, 95
Montelius, Oskar, 48, 54
Moundbuilders, 3–6
Mound Builders of Ancient America: The Archaeology of a Myth (Silverberg), 4
Mounds, Hopewell, 3–6, 29–36
Mount Browne, 59
Münnich, Karl Otto, 52
Mycenae, 48, 49, 53

National Institute of Anthropology (Mexico), 85
Nazca markings, 13–16, 69–76
Neolithic period
  dating of, 51
  in Egypt, 83
  and European megalithic monuments, 48, 63–66
Newark Works, as Hopewell site, 29–30
Newgrange, 58, 59, 62–65
Newham, C.A., 11
Nile River, 20, 78–84

Oaxaca, 86, 95
Obsidian
  in Hopewell mounds, 31
  in Mexico, 22, 85
Ohio, Hopewell culture in, 3–5, 29–36
Olmecs, 85, 86
Orkney, megalithic monuments in, 59
Our Inheritance in the Great Pyramid (Smyth), 18
Owen, George, 60

Paddock, John, 93
Palestine, stone monuments in, 56
Pampa Colorada, 69–73, 75–76
Pauli, Wolfgang, 16–17
Pauwels, Louis, 14, 17
Pearls, in Hopewell mounds, 31
Peet, T.E., 56
Persia, stone monuments in, 56
Peru, Nazca markings in, 13, 69–76
Petrie, Flinders, 18, 78
Pharaohs, tombs of, 20, 78–84
Pi (π), 19
Piggott, Stuart, 8
Pinus aristata. *See* Bristlecone pine trees
Pleiades, constellation, 22
Population growth, Nazca drawings affecting, 71, 73
Portugal, stone chamber tombs in, 59, 63, 64
Presely Mountains, in Wales, 42
Prufer, Olaf, 3, 5, 29–36
Pseudoarchaeology, vs. archaeology, 1–24
Pyramid of the Moon, 21, 86, 91, 94
Pyramid of the Sun, 21–23, 85, 91, 92
Pyramids
  of Egypt, 1, 17–21
  in Mexico, 21–23, 85–95
  in Peru, 70
  and role of diffusion, 1, 23
Pyramids of Egypt, The (Edwards), 20

Quetzalcoatl, Temple of, 86–88, 94
Quibell, J.E., 78
Quipu, 76

Radiocarbon dating
  archaeological use of, 3
  for Hopewell cult, 29, 34
  for Nazca drawings, 70
  for prehistoric Europe, 47–55
Redman, Charles L., 2
Reiche, Maria, 13–16, 69, 73, 75
Religious significance
  of Egyptian pyramids, 22
  of European megaliths, 65–66
  of Hopewell mounds, 31–32, 36
  of Maltese stone monuments, 49, 59, 62, 63
  of Mesoamerican pyramids, 22, 85–95
  of Stonehenge, 13, 40, 45
Renfrew, Colin, 9–10, 47–55
Riddle of the Pyramids, The (Mendelssohn), 20
Ritual significance, of Nazca markings, 16, 73–75. *See also* Burial sites; Religious significance
Rough Stone Monuments (Peet), 56
Rowe, John H., 70
Rude Stone Monuments in All Countries (Fergusson), 8, 56

Sagan, Carl, 12
Sakkara, 78–80, 82, 83
Sanders, William T., 86, 93
Sarcophagus, 80
Sarsen stones, at Stonehenge, 11, 41–42, 44, 61
Sawyer, Alan, 16
Scandinavia, megalithic monuments in, 59, 61, 64
Schulman, Edmund, 52
Scientific method, employed by archaeologists, 3
Scioto tradition, 32, 36
Scott, Stuart D., 7
Secrets of the Great Pyramid (Tompkins), 17
Seip site, of Hopewell cult, 29
Séjourné, Laurette, 89
Shetrone, Henry C., 4
Silverberg, Robert, 4
Siret, Henri, 48
Siret, Louis, 48
Smith, G. Elliot, 56, 63
Smith, Sir Grafton, 48
Smyth, Charles Piazzi, 18
Snow, Dean R., 69, 70
Spain
  "Copper Age" of, 48
  and cultural diffusion, 47
  stone monuments in, 59, 61, 63, 64, 66
Station stone, at Stonehenge, 10
Statue menhir, 56, 59
Stenness, 59
Step pyramids, 20
Stone, J.F.S., 8
Stone Age, 47
Stonehenge
  astronomical aspects of, 11–13, 61
  dating of, 8–10, 44, 56, 57, 63
  description of, 39–45
  diffusion vs. independent invention of, 10, 53
  myths regarding, 8, 40
  periods of construction of, 10–11, 63
  purposes of, 65

Stonehenge (Atkinson), 8
Stonehenge and Its Environs, 10
Stonehenge and Other British Stone Monuments Astronomically Considered (Lockyer), 11
Stonehenge Decoded (Hawkins),11, 61
Storage centers, Nazca drawings affecting, 71, 73, 76
Story, Ronald, 19
Street of the Dead, 86–87, 93
Strong, W. Duncan, 70
Stukeley, William, 40, 45
Sudan, stone monuments in, 56
Suess, Hans E., 50, 52–53, 63

Table stone, 60
Tauber, Henrik, 52
Temple of Quetzalcoatl, 86, 87, 88, 94
Temples. *See also* Religious significance
  of Malta, 49, 59, 62, 63
  Mesoamerican pyramids as, 22, 85–95
  of Neolithic people, 65–66
  vs. tombs, 61
Teotihuacán pyramids, 1, 17, 21–23, 85–95
Thermoluminescence dating, 63
Thom, A.S., 11, 59, 61
Thomas, Cyrus, 4
Thomsen, C.J., 47
Tikal, 92, 94
Tomb. *See* Burial sites
Tompkins, Peter, 17, 18
Tree-ring calibration. *See* Bristlecone pine trees
Trigger, Bruce, 7
Trimble, Virginia, 19
Troy, Bronze Age artifacts from, 49
Turner site, of Hopewell cult, 31, 32

Uadji (Egyptian pharaoh), 79, 82
Udimu (Egyptian pharaoh), 78, 83
UFOs, 12–13, 14, 56
Urton, Gary, 15

Valley of Mexico, 85, 88, 93
Valley of Puebla, 85, 88
Vinča culture, 51, 53
Von Däniken, Erich, 13–16, 19, 56

Wales
  megalithic monument in, 60
  Stonehenge blue stone from, 12, 42, 43, 61
White, Peter, 13, 17, 18, 19
Willey, Gordon R., 23, 70
Williams, Carlos, 76
Willis, Eric H., 52
Wilson, Clifford, 17
Woodhenges, 64
Woodland culture, 32, 35–36

Xesspe, Toribio Mejía, 69

Y Hole, at Stonehenge, 11, 41, 43, 44
Yugoslavia, Neolithic artifacts from, 49

Z Hole, at Stonehenge, 11, 41, 43, 44
Zuidema, R. Tom, 74